GET RICH IN 5 HOURS

How to Go from Being Poor to Being Rich

JOSEPH HERBERT

GetRichIn5Hours
Joseph Herbert
www.GetRichIn5Hours.com
Joe@GetRichIn5Hours.com

ISBN: 978-1-7341332-0-2 (Paperback)
ISBN: 978-1-7341332-1-9 (eBook)

Library of Congress Control Number: 2019918467

City of Publication: Erie, PA

Front and back cover design and image by Joseph Herbert
Book design by Joseph Herbert

First Printing edition 2020

ACKNOWLEDGEMENTS

To my parents for never giving up on me. I know I made your life very difficult at times. Thank you for always telling me I could do better. Thank you for being so selfless and working hard all your lives so my brother, sisters and I could have a better life. I have your incredible work ethic. I will never forget what you did for me. My mother always told me to "Never settle for anything in life." I never forgot she said that.

Thank you to my wife for all her support and faith in me to succeed. Thank you to Molly, Flower and Edy for always going crazy when I get home. It is the best feeling in the world.

I am so thankful for all the great families who lived on 21st street when I was growing up. All of you had a great positive influence on me. Every day that goes by I realize how critical you all are to my success.

I want to thank my first business partners for getting me involved in real estate investing. Thank you to all my Mastermind friends for allowing me to "never be the smartest person in the room."

I am saving the best for last. Thank you to my Lord for giving me such a blessed life and allowing me to be in a place where I can help other people have a better life.

Molly

Flower

Edy

TABLE OF CONTENTS

PREFACE

The people who typically inspire authors to write books are usually close to the author, like a parent, spouse or child. Sometimes it is a mentor or business partner or a close friend. My inspiration comes from a completely different group of people: all the people out there whom I have never met, who are struggling every day to just maintain what they have in life.

I wrote this book because so many people today are stuck in a life of financial misery. Being mired in debt and barely making ends meet is a life of stress and worry. Today most people do not possess the beliefs, decisions, mindset, goals, daily habits, and environment that allow them to think, act and live like a rich person and enjoy financial freedom. This mindset is not taught in any school. A bigger problem is most people do not understand what it takes to change their life to acquire these skills and tools. Without a book like this or professional help, most people will not be able to identify and understand the social, emotional, educational and financial barriers that are holding them back or how to remove these barriers.

It is impossible to change your financial situation without changing most aspects of your life. Changing your life must come first if you want to change your net worth and income. It is not the other way around. You don't become wealthy and rich first and then decide to make some changes. The only time the money comes before change is if you win a hefty sum, you inherit the money, or you steal it. I guarantee your life will not change if you acquire money by these methods. Because your mindset has not changed first, you will not like what happens afterwards. You won't have the money very long and you may suffer other consequences.

Like many people in this country today, I was living paycheck-to-paycheck, weekend to weekend, speeding ticket to speeding ticket and car repair to car repair. I could not stand my boss or my job. Every day I got out of bed having no control over how my day would unfold; I just hoped I got lucky and "caught a break" that day. I dreaded Sunday evenings because I knew I had to go to work the next day. Once the workweek started, I could not wait until Friday at 5 p.m.

I was the king of failure. I could write an entire book on my mistakes. I know exactly what it is like to fail and struggle and not know what to do to change things. I have been kicked to the curb so many times in life that at one point I thought I was a stunt man. I was sent home regularly for bad behavior when I was in grade school, I almost flunked out of high school and I flunked out of college after one year. My first business partnership failed after twelve years and I wound up sick and broke.

By the time I was fifty, I was in debt and had lost all the money I earned over twenty-five years of working and investing. I had just spent five days in the hospital with severe ulcerative colitis and I had the worst negative attitude of anyone you will ever meet. I had to sell my condo because I could no longer afford the monthly payment.

So why should you read my book? What makes me the right person to write a book like this? The reason is because if a person like me figured out how to learn from my mistakes, realize there is a better way to live my life, find that better way and greatly prosper from it personally and financially, you might want to listen up.

If you have never been face-down in a mud puddle, completely broke and questioning yourself and who your friends are then you shouldn't be giving advice to people who are in that situation. I have been in that mud puddle. I've been poor and broke. I've made lots of money and lost it. I spent time doubting myself, analyzing my past, blaming everyone else except myself and dwelling on my regrets. To sum it up, I have been there, I know what it is like and I know how to change it.

Today I own a successful real estate brokerage, numerous cash flow producing rental properties, an online education company and I am a self-published author. Today on a scale of one to ten I would rate my life a ten and it is getting better every day. I believe the turnaround in my happiness, health, love life, wealth and future growth has been nothing short of miraculous.

The simple fact that I started out with nothing, made every mistake in the book, was completely unaware of how I was making decisions and still figured out how to turn it around and build and live a better life, makes me the perfect person to write this book. If I can turn my life around and be successful, then you can too.

The good news is I am here with this awesome book to help you learn from both my mistakes and my success, so you don't have to go through what I went through. Trial and error and learning the hard way are not good paths for success and becoming rich. My biggest motivation for writing this book was the many times I wished someone had shared a book like this with me while I was struggling to succeed in life. I owed it to the universe to put this book together for people like you, so you can enjoy the incredible life I am enjoying.

It is human nature to want to share something spectacular that has happened to you. Think about the following scenarios. When fishermen catch a trophy fish, they can't wait to tell their fishing buddies. When you hit a hole in one in golf you call your friends right away and share every detail of how it happened. When you hit the lottery, you run home and tell your spouse. When I had my "awakening" and realized how to start being rich, it was like hitting the lottery. The day I started studying these principles and beliefs and applying them to my own life, my enthusiasm to change my life for the better was all I could think about and my attitude shot through the roof. I had won a lottery more valuable than any money lottery: a priceless lifetime gift of exploring and achieving everything life offers. My happiness, love life, wealth and health have been increasing and improving ever since this discovery.

Ever since my life has changed so dramatically for the better it has become very important to me that I am given the chance to help people like you change your life for the better. I am totally committed to help you achieve your maximum potential and obtain and maintain success in all areas of your life. Please give me your trust and focus and I promise to start you down the path of self-discovery and enjoyment of all that life offers. I will do everything in my power to help you make your life better.

INTRODUCTION

Can anyone really get rich in five hours? Does that sound too good to be true? What an absurd proposition! I believe you can get rich in five hours and that is why I wrote this book. I will prove it to you as you read this book. For me to prove it, you must read this book in its entirety.

Let's examine the proposition of getting rich in five hours. First you must understand what the definition of being rich is. If you ask a hundred people what it would take to make them rich, 99 out of a hundred would respond that it would take a large amount of money. For these people to get rich in five hours, they would have to rob a bank, inherit a lot of money, hit the lottery, or invent something nobody has ever thought of before.

The single biggest reason 99% of our population is not rich is because their definition of being rich means acquiring a lot of money, owning a luxury car, or having a huge house. If you think obtaining a lot of money is the measure of wealth and riches, you are mistaken. Money alone does not make a person rich. If you are truly rich, you can generate sources of money any time you want. You will never be dependent on crime or an event of great luck to acquire money. Once you have the mindset and belief systems of a wealthy person, you can't help but get rich. The money will follow you.

There is nothing more powerful than being able to think, act, and live like a successful rich person. In fact, the minute you understand the laws, beliefs, and rules of success and wealth, you will become a rich person. The effect on your life is instant and never ends if you maintain and practice these rules and beliefs.

Have you ever heard the proverb, *"Give a man a fish*

and you feed him for a day? Teach a man to fish and he can feed himself for life"?

This saying couldn't be more accurate when it comes to money and wealth. How many stories have you heard in the news about people who win millions of dollars in the lottery only to be broke or worse off a few years later? I truly believe if I gave most poor people a check for a million dollars today, and they did not change their habits or belief systems, most of the money (if not all of it) would be gone in three to five years.

It has been said by numerous entrepreneurs, financial analysts, politicians, and professors that If you took all the money away from the wealthiest people in the world and gave it to the poorest people in the world, within five years or less all that money would be back in the hands of the richest people. This is not because rich people are crooks. It is only because of the way rich people think and the way poor people think. Being wealthy is a state of mind.

I recently read a study in Forbes magazine of several hundred billionaires. The study was trying to determine what traits, if any, were shared by all billionaires. One of the most common traits of billionaires is that they lost all their money at some point in time but recovered from their losses and became billionaires again. This illustrates the difference in paradigm between those who have a success mindset versus those who do not. It came down to the belief systems they held, not how much money they had. Even though they lost their money, they believed they could get it back—and they did.

There are several life-changing benefits of being able to think like a rich person. First and foremost, you become able to help other people in ways you were not aware of before. This alone is worth the time and effort to become rich. Zig Ziglar said it best: *"You can have anything you want in life if you help enough other people get what they want out of life.*"

The second very enjoyable benefit is financial freedom. For me, this is the ability to do what I want, when I want, and where I want. It is having the ability to help my loved ones in a time of need. It is never having to worry about paying bills again. It is having the time and money to travel and enjoy life. It is not having to worry about how I am going to retire. It is not having to worry about a downturn in life because I know I have the proper savings and insurance in place. Helping people obtain and maintain this financial freedom is one of the main reasons I decided to write this book. Financial freedom is one of the best feelings in the world.

When I was growing up my parents lived paycheck-to-paycheck and they often fought with each other about their lack of money. I did not have any friends or family members who were rich or successful entrepreneurs. The multi-billionaire stock market guru, Warren Buffet, said, "*It is okay to learn from mistakes, just make sure they are someone else's.*" Unfortunately, I had to figure things out the hard way, by trial and error. This book is about helping you avoid the years of mistakes, trial, and error it takes to become rich. I can't tell you how many times I have said to myself, "*I wish someone had shared this knowledge and wisdom with me when I was younger.*" If someone handed me this book 30 years ago, my life would have changed dramatically.

I have been poor, and I have been financially free. I will choose financial freedom over being poor every day. I had my days when I was scraping coins out of my car seat to buy another gallon of gas. When I was in college, I hitchhiked back and forth from Rochester, NY, to Erie, PA, to visit my family on the weekends.

David, Dad, and Myself

One of the most painful memories I have in life is when my brother died at the age of 30. It was extremely painful to lose my brother at such a young age. This painful loss for my family and I was compounded by the fact that we were not by his side when he passed away. My brother was living in Washington, DC, and we knew he was very ill. He had just been rushed to the hospital and was not given long to live. My parents were struggling financially at that time. Because of our financial situation, we could not just hop on a plane or jump in a car and rush to him. We had one older, rundown car and it would not make the trip to be with him. Before we could figure out how to get to Washington, he died alone in a hospital bed without us by his side. I will never forget that. I can't explain to you the feeling of helplessness my family experienced that day, all because of the lack of money. I will never let myself or my family be poor again. I refuse to ever live paycheck-to-paycheck again or be in a position where I can't be there for my family in a time of need.

First let me say I love and respect my mother and father very much. My parents are two of the most self-less people I know. They both had incredible work ethics. My siblings and I were truly blessed to have them as our parents. I would not change that for anything. My father is my fishing and sports watching buddy. When I was growing up, he never put his personal needs before the needs of his family. My mother was super hardworking and the most giving person I have ever met. She was an angel. I want to say this because, going forward in this book, I might seem disrespectful towards my parents with some of my perspectives and stories. I respect my parents, but I need to tell the truth about my family background to communicate the enormous effect the knowledge in this book has had on my life.

Mom and Dad

My father was a very hardworking person. For most of my youth, he had two jobs just to make ends meet. He did not finish high school and never had anyone in his life to help him with money, business, or a positive mindset. As a child, his household had a culture of tough love. It is not an accident my father had a very negative outlook on life. No matter what went wrong with my father's life, it was instantly someone else's fault. I watched my father make one bad personal and business decision after the next. His life never changed financially or socially.

My father spent 20 some years working at the A&P grocery store as a butcher and produce department manager. Two years before he was eligible for a full pension, he left his job at the grocery store to open a fishing tackle shop, and named it the Summit Sports Store. He purchased an existing inventory of another fishing tackle store and went into business for himself. Unfortunately, the inventory he purchased was obsolete and he paid thousands of dollars more than it was worth. Eventually, my father failed in the fishing store venture and had to close his doors.

Summit Sport Store

Shortly after my father's store closed, the sheriff showed up at our house to post a foreclosure notice. Fortunately, my mother knew the sheriff and talked him into coming back in a few weeks. He never came back so I am guessing my mother borrowed some money from her siblings and caught up on the mortgage.

My mother worked in the same shoe store for minimum wage for over 40 years. It was the only job she ever had. She always put that store before her personal life and made countless sacrifices with her time and income so the shoe store could succeed. I remember when she had her 25-year anniversary as an employee, the owner came over our house and gave her a gift of a new watch. My mother cried when she opened the gift. She wept like a person who had just hit the lottery. I couldn't believe my mother thought a $50 watch was a great reward for 25 years of personal sacrifice running this man's shoe store for him. After she received the watch, my mother worked another 15 years for the same employer. After 40 years in the same job she had no ownership interest, no stock options, no 401K, and no pension.

Unfortunately, my mother passed away from her eight-year battle with cancer at the age of 63. She worked until the day she died and had no money when she passed away. It was heartbreaking on so many levels.

Belief systems and perspectives are inherited from our environment and mostly from our parents. My parents did not have the mindset, belief systems, or knowledge of rich people. As I grew up, neither did I. I turned out just like my father when it came to problem solving, conflict resolution, and building relationships. I blamed everyone else but myself for what happened to me. I did not stick with anything I started. I was great at criticizing others. I was sent home from grade school at least once a week for bad behavior. I was almost held back in high school and I flunked out of college after one year. I could go on for several pages about all the foolish mistakes I made but I think you get the picture. My life was lived in the moment without a single thought about even the second half of the day I was in.

After I was kicked out of college, I worked for a construction company for a couple years as a laborer. It was backbreaking work. By now, the friends I grew up with were in their third and fourth year of college. I was growing apart from them because they were maturing, getting smarter, and making new friends. We didn't have much in common anymore. I stayed the same and I did not like it. Between busting butt at my construction job and watching my friends succeed in life, I knew I had to go back to college.

I give my mother credit for constantly preaching to

my siblings and me about staying in school and going to college. The other fortunate decision my parents made when I was six years old was to move to a neighborhood with numerous good families. This proved to be a lifesaver for me. If not for the decision to move to the neighborhood we lived in I would not have been surrounded by kids who went on to college. Later in this book, I will talk about how critical it is to surround yourself with successful people. This childhood experience of growing up with kids who wanted to go to college was my first lesson in what I call the principle for success. A lesson I learned completely by accident because of the house my parents purchased.

Let me fast-forward to the day of my epiphany about changing my life. I call it "The Switch." It was the day the light switch went on in my mind about how I was living my life up to that day. Something happened to me that made me realize I had to completely change my belief systems and who I was spending my time with. After college, one of my best friends, his brother, father, and I opened a bar and restaurant. At first it was an enormous success. We started purchasing rental properties with the profits from the bar and restaurant. Then we opened a nightclub. We purchased a big boat and a beach house. We had pockets full of cash and plenty of friends. Because my basic belief systems had not changed at all, I was a poor kid living a rich guy's lifestyle. As the saying goes, I was given a fish (lots of cash), but I hadn't learned how to fish. We were living like rock stars. Unfortunately, within ten years our businesses were all losing money and I had sold all my rental properties to maintain them. I was living paycheck-to-paycheck and lost all the equity I had accumulated from twenty years of post-college efforts. I was sick from all the stress and had severe stomach problems. I hated my daytime job as a software developer, and my girlfriend of eight years had just dumped me for another guy. My business partners and I were upside down cash flow-wise, fighting with each other, and going through a business divorce. I wound up in the hospital for five days with a bunch of tubes coming out of me wondering what the hell went wrong. I had to sell my condo because I could not afford the mortgage payments any longer. I wound up living in an apartment above a TV repair shop, fifteen feet from a very busy road with tractor-trailer trucks and ambulances flying by my bedroom window every night.

I spent most of my evenings sitting on the couch analyzing my life. How could I be penniless after a great college education, working in the corporate world for twenty years, owning two businesses, and purchasing numerous rental properties?

How could both of my parents have no equity in their home, no money in the bank, no pension, and zero assets after working incredibly hard for 40 years? My parents were never late to work. They never called off sick. They never got fired. They did not steal from their employers. They always followed orders and treated the customers well. I can say the same for me. I was very hardworking. I always showed up on time. I did not steal from my employers. How could I be penniless after so much hard work and investing?

The answer to this question is very simple. The reason this all happened to my parents and me was because we did not know how to think like wealthy successful people. We did not understand the belief systems, mindset, knowledge, habits, and tools used to build and maintain wealth. It is truly that simple. The difference between our lives and the lives of people who do not fail, when it comes to financial freedom, was the information and beliefs we used to make social, financial, and health decisions on a regular basis. It was a simple matter of knowing what to do and what not to do with our time, money, mindset, knowledge, social circle, and health.

After I lost all my money and had to sell all my real estate, a couple of events happened that turned things around for me in a huge way. While I was sitting on my couch one evening sulking about my losses and nursing my bad health, the first episode of *The Apprentice* reality show was airing on television. The show featured a handpicked group of young professionals trying to win a one-year apprenticeship working for a billionaire entrepreneur. During the show, the Billionaire had sidebar conversations with the camera. He would talk about what was important to becoming successful. A consistent theme from him was surrounding yourself with successful people. He also talked about hiring talent and always pursuing something you love doing. Later in this book, I will expand on those principles for success and many more. Whether you like this billionaire entrepreneur or not, his comments flipped a switch in my mind and made me realize how little thought I gave to who I was associating with. It made me think about what I was doing for a living and if I loved what I was doing. My mind went crazy about the prospect that I could have an impact on the outcome of my life by making conscious decisions about these things.

About this same time, a second pivotal event occurred. A friend and colleague gave me a personal improvement audio recording by a speaker named Earl Nightingale. It was outwardly apparent that I was down on life and not very happy about anything at that time. The friend took notice of my bad attitude and felt the recording would do me some good. The audio recording was called, *The Strangest Secret*. The central message in the audio recording is "We become what we think about." I soon learned that the way people think is the only difference between being poor or becoming rich. The recording has sent me on a never-ending journey to pursue personal growth, success, and wealth. It is still one of my favorite audio recordings to listen to. It changed my life forever because it changed the way I was thinking. Thank you, Dan O.!

Today it is still the most popular mindset to go to school so you can get a job. We are not taught to educate ourselves after our formal education. The famous author and motivational speaker, Zig Ziglar, said it best: *"Your formal education will get you a job. Your self-education will make you a fortune."* Self-education is one of the habits that separates rich people from everyone else. This one habit will lead you to all the wisdom and knowledge you will ever need to truly become rich.

Today the middle class and the lifestyle of being an employee are under siege and may be dying a slow death. We now have a demographic in our society that the media refers to as the Working Poor. This is a sector of our society that works for money but lives in poverty because their income is barely enough to live on. The middle class and this working poor class are becoming poorer each day because their income never goes up, but the cost of food, housing, transportation, insurance, education, and health care continue to rise every year. The next 10-15 years are going to usher in some amazing technological advancements such as robots, automation and artificial intelligence. It remains to be seen how this will affect employees from the middle class and working poor, but most predictions are that 30-40% of all jobs performed by humans will be gone. It is more important than ever to learn how to think like a rich person if you want to not only survive financially, but also to prosper and grow toward financial independence.

When I was working in the corporate world as an electrical engineer, I heard a statement about companies that now applies to the individual as well. *"You either grow or you die."* As harsh as that sounds, the days of performing the same job for 30 years and getting your pension or social security check are over. The household and per capita income of middle-class employees has not grown. It has shrunk over the past 100 years due to corporate greed and overpaid CEOs. Social Security income is projected to be reduced by as much as 25% by the United States Federal government. With this new wave of technology impacting every aspect of your lives, I believe the middle class is going to take another hit. Now is the time to circle your financial wagons.

How to Get Rich in 5 Hours is a book for people who are serious about taking a quantum leap forward in changing their financial place in life. The goal of this book is to end your thinking and acting like an employee and transform your thinking, beliefs, and decision making to that of a rich person. I will outline what changes you will need to make to overcome the social, emotional, psychological, and financial barriers that keep people from becoming rich. This book is the foundation of the laws for wealth and a roadmap to changing the way you view money and wealth. If the wisdom and beliefs in this book are used correctly and consistently, you are guaranteed to start an exciting journey towards financial freedom and prosperity. I know this to be true because all the information in this book has transformed my mind, beliefs, daily decisions, number of assets I own, cash flow and bank account from that of a poor person to a rich person. I hope this book flips the switch in your conscious and subconscious mind to forever change your life. You deserve to have a healthy and prosperous life.

WHAT IT MEANS TO BE RICH

WHAT IT MEANS TO BE RICH

What does it mean to you to be rich? If you ask a hundred people what their definition of wealth is, you will get a hundred different answers. Most of the answers will contain statements about acquiring a large amount of money, owning a big house, buying a luxury car, partying on a yacht, or not having to work anymore.

I want to be very clear about three critical premises you must understand and believe if you are going to become rich.

1. *Being rich has absolutely nothing to do with the amount of money a person has or receives or if they own expensive things.*

2. *Only working smart and hard over time bringing value to other people will change the amount of money a person regularly earns and keeps.*

3. *If you want to become rich and stay rich, you must learn how to leverage your six Life Assets.*

Let's examine the first premise of how being rich has absolutely nothing to do with the amount of money a person has or receives or if they own expensive things. The true meaning of being rich is defined by a person's quality of life, not by amounts of money or luxury possessions. Tai Lopez, one of today's online personal improvement gurus, defines success as having "health, wealth, love and happiness." He is not too far off with that simple definition.

Based on this view of being rich, you probably want to stop reading this book. As Tom Cruise said in the movie, *Jerry Maguire*, "Show me the money!" You probably want me to show you the money right now, not the quality of life.

During my journey to alter my mindset, habits, decisions, income, and net worth, I became aware of these two facts:

1. If I were to give most people a large sum of money, an expensive home, and a luxury car, it would not change their lives and they would not be rich.

2. If a person reads this book and applies the knowledge, beliefs, wisdom, and mindset in the following pages, that person will have the greatest chance of changing their life and becoming and staying rich.

Please read the quote below several times. This is another basic concept you must understand.

"Rich people don't live their lives the way they do because they have a lot of money. Rich people have a lot of money because of the way they live their lives."

When most of society views rich people enjoying the best things in life, they assume that is the benefit of having a lot of money. Rich people know that the money they have in their possession does not truly belong to them. Because of the way they think, act, speak, and bring value to other people, the world has allowed rich people to control large sums of money. Rich people use this money to enrich their own lives and empower themselves to help other people. That is why rich people don't focus on the amount of money they control. Rich people have confidence knowing that if they take care of money and use it to help other people, their own lives will be enriched. They know more money will flow to them every day.

Money flows to people who take care of it, treat it with care, and do good things with it. Money wants to be respected, valued, taken care of, and used to benefit others. It will flow in abundance to those who use it to do the right thing.

You can help a person cross the street or let a person get in line in front of you. I highly encourage you to do these types of courteous and gracious gestures every day, whenever the chance presents itself. The world needs a lot more of this type of courtesy. Being nice to other people is also good for your immune system and emotional outlook on life. I feel great whenever I let another driver pull out in front of me or when I hold the door for another person and let them go ahead of me.

When you are rich, you can help people on a much larger scale than just holding the door for them. You can use your money to open a school to teach under-privileged children about investing and entrepreneurial skills. You can donate money to a non-profit organization that helps homeless people. You can open a soup kitchen for hungry people. You can give tuition scholarships to under-privileged children to help pay for their post-high school education. Doing small favors is nice and we need more of it, but a rich person with money can have a deeper, more impactful, and longer lasting effect on people than simply holding a door for someone.

Below is a list of the qualities and traits of a rich person. Whenever I talk about a rich person from this point forward, I am talking about a person who:

- is honest and ethical.
- respects and loves themselves and the people they

surround themselves with.

- is well-liked by their friends, family, clients, employees, and customers.
- values their health and lives a healthy lifestyle.
- shows up on time and does what they say they are going to do.
- holds themselves accountable for their actions and the outcome of their efforts.
- works smart and hard over time to build their wealth and passive income.
- uses their services and products to bring value to other people.
- charges a fair price for their goods and services.
- owns assets like rental property, stocks, mutual funds, and businesses.
- avoids bad debt.
- works on things they are passionate about.
- knows their strengths and weaknesses.
- knows how to use leverage.
- can quit their day job because their investments provide enough passive income to support their standard of living and allow them to continue to acquire additional investments.
- constantly pursues change and personal growth by reading, watching, and listening to positive educational content.
- always networks with other prosperous people.
- is constantly looking for their next mentor or coach.
- attends seminars and conferences to learn more about investing.
- acquires new skills, expands their field of expertise, or learns about a new discipline they are interested in

pursuing.

Notice that in the list of the above there is no mention of a large amount of money, an expensive house, luxury cars, or a big boat. Again, I want to reinforce the premise that being rich has absolutely nothing to do with the amount of money a person has.

Large sums of money are acquired and lost all the time. Living like the rich person described in the list above will allow you to consistently acquire and keep money, treat it with care, and do meaningful things with it.

A second concept I will talk about over and over in this book is that only working smart and hard over time bringing value to other people will change the amount of money a person regularly earns and keeps.

This version of getting rich works for everyone who employs it. Trying to get a lot of money right away with no effort is a plan that works for very few people. If you plan on acquiring a lot of money from inheritance, gambling, or crime, you are going to be disappointed.

Casino gamblers typically lose between $100,000,000 to $200,000,000 annually. The least wealthy group of families receive on average about $6,100 in inheritance. People in the income bracket $25,000 to $250,000 a year inherit anywhere from $15,000 to $50,000. It is difficult for a person to spend the remainder of their life living on $50,000, which is not enough money to allow a person to quit their job and retire. Only the wealthiest 1% of families receives on average about $2.7 million in inheritance.

As far as crime goes, you might get away with stealing money or robbing houses for a brief amount of time, but you will soon wind up in jail. The old saying, "crime doesn't pay," has been around for a long time for a reason. Crime is not an option for getting rich.

If you watch YouTube videos about wealth building, success, and personal improvement, all these videos have ads at the beginning of them showing people who claim to have gotten rich overnight. These overnight millionaires want you to buy their Internet marketing plans or their secret formulas that promise you will be rich in months. The setting for these ads is a gorgeous tropical island or a multi-million-dollar house with an expensive sports car in the driveway. The reason they present their products this way is because, as I mentioned earlier, so many people think being rich is all about having luxury cars, a huge house, and an expensive boat.

This type of product and marketing brings no value to anyone. These Internet multi-level or network marketing schemes aren't selling a service or a product. The way these people are getting rich is by selling you their get-rich-quick scheme on the Internet. Their system is all about you selling the same false promise to another poor sucker. Most of these so-called lifestyle entrepreneurs who are professing to have "made it" will be broke in two to five years because they don't have a product or service that brings any value to anyone. If these secret get-rich ideas were really that easy and fast, then everyone would be rich.

Only working smart and hard over time bringing value to other people will change the amount of money a person regularly earns or has in the bank. To me, being wealthy means having the opportunity to bring value to other people through my products and services. I can take care of my family in any situation that life throws at me. I work where I want, when I want, doing what I love to do. My money works for me instead of me working for money because I have harnessed my six Life Assets.

The third premise of this book is, if you want to become rich and stay rich, you must learn how to leverage your six Life Assets. Every person on the planet has the same six Life Assets. I believe the six Life Assets are superpowers. That might sound crazy at first, but if you knew how much my life has turned around and continues to improve physically, emotionally, and financially because of my use of them, you would view them this way, too.

The Six Life Assets are:

1. Mindset.
2. People.
3. Time.
4. Knowledge.
5. Money.
6. Health.

According to the website, Investopedia: "*An asset is a resource with economic value that an individual, corporation, or country owns or controls with the expectation that it will provide a future benefit. Assets are reported on a company's balance sheet and are bought or created to increase a firm's value or benefit the firm's operations. An asset can be thought of as something that, in the future, can generate cash flow, reduce expenses, or improve sales, regardless of whether it's manufacturing equipment or a patent.*"

Examples of the Investopedia assets are physical property like real estate, cash in the bank, inventory, accounts receivable, stocks, and mutual funds.

However, I do not classify these types of assets as Life Assets because they do not exist in every person's life. For an asset to be one of the six Life Assets, it must exist in every person's life, have a major impact on the quality of their life, and be necessary to become and stay rich.

All of us, no matter where we live, how old we are, or whether we're already rich or still poor, have the power to benefit from our six Life Assets. If we take the time to understand these Assets and learn how to use them properly, they can provide us with great economic value and a huge future benefit.

My mindset is one of extreme confidence, abundance, and sharing. I feel the law of attraction working for me every day. My knowledge about health, family, business, and investing grows every day. The number of relationships I have with positive successful people increases daily. My income increases every year and my portfolio of real estate is multiplying. Today my health is the best it has been in the past 20 years. I go to bed every night so thankful for the awesome day I had, and I can't wait to wake up the next day because I know I am in total control of my destiny.

Real Estate Investment Properties

I purchased a 10-unit office building and a six-unit apartment building in just the past 60 days. My real estate brokerage team is poised to double in size this year. My marriage with my wife is the strongest it has ever been. My tennis game is better than any other time in my life. I started working out with free weights again after 15 years of being absent from the gym. This is all happening for me because I guard and leverage my six Life Assets.

Most people have no idea they possess these Life Assets and that they are superpowers. If not used wisely, these assets can also have a negative effect on one's life. As

I go through life and encounter people who are not doing well, I can see how their current quality of life is directly related to how they are not using their Life Assets. The correlation between their quality of life and how they are wasting their Life Assets is extremely obvious to me. If they only knew how their life would completely turn around for the better if they would just stop wasting these superpowers. The goal of this book is to make people aware of what the six Life Assets are, how valuable they are, how to gain control of them, and how to use them to become rich.

The Life Assets work in concert with each other. Each asset can help develop, support, and increase the other assets. If any asset is not used carefully or wasted, it can reduce the value of the other assets. If you don't take care to have good health, then you won't have the energy to change your life. If you continue to waste time, then you can't grow your mindset or knowledge. If you stay broke and in debt, it will be hard to afford things like self-education or quality food to maintain energy and good health.

The first Asset we will explore is Mindset. This is an incredible Life Asset. A person's mindset can be positive, confident, trusting, and growth-oriented. It can also be negative, fearful, dishonest, and mistrusting. Either way, that person has a mindset. Mindset probably has the biggest effect on how well you leverage the other Assets because it is formed by your beliefs.

Every person on the planet has a set of beliefs, the ability to make decisions, self-esteem, confidence, a view of life, and a comfort zone. Some people are more positive and confident than other people. Some people are negative, fearful, and mistrusting.

Unfortunately, most people do not understand how

valuable their mindset is and how much it is impacting their life. Your mindset impacts your health, relationships, career, income, and net worth every day. You cannot become and stay rich without the mindset of a rich person. The chapter on mindset will explore techniques to change your outlook on life, reduce your fears, expand your comfort zone, and get the law of attraction working for you.

The second Life Asset is People. People are a Life Asset because we all know people. Every person knows or has known some other people in their life. A relative, neighbor, coworker, or friend. Even the poorest and loneliest person on the planet knows someone else. Every person on the planet started out with two parents.

The effect that people have on our lives cannot be overstated. The influence people have on our lives can be very powerful. I have learned over the course of my life how just one person can have an exponential impact on another person's life. One great mentor or coach can lift a person to new heights. One negative toxic person can destroy another person's life. You cannot become and stay rich without surrounding yourself with the right people. People are a tremendous Life Asset.

Time is the third Life Asset because it exists in every person's life. In fact, time is the one Asset we all get the same amount of. We all get 24 hours in each day. Nothing more and nothing less. It doesn't matter where you live or how rich or poor you are. Everyone gets 24 hours per day. One of the biggest differences between rich people and people who are not rich is that rich people do things with their time that most other people do not. How you manage your time determines how rich you become. Time is one of the most valuable Life Assets. Later in the book, I will break down where all our time goes and give suggestions about how to recapture your time. I will give you examples of how rich people avoid wasting time and what they do with their time that has such a huge impact on their ability to become and stay rich.

Knowledge is the fourth Life Asset. Every person has knowledge about something. Even the most uneducated and most inexperienced person knows something. If the only thing you knew were your name and where you were born, that is still a form of knowledge. Most people view learning and self-education as a chore and only necessary to get a job. Once they get a job, they stop learning. Rich people are life-long learners. They view knowledge and education as fun, fulfilling, and part of their everyday quest for growth. Rich people know they must continue to learn if they want to stay rich and even grow their net worth and income. Rich people are not afraid to spend money on self-education to help them become rich. Most people who are not rich wouldn't even think about spending money on self-education unless it was going to help them get a pay raise or another job. Ever since I made self-education a regular part of my life, my income and net worth have continued to grow. Knowledge is a critical Life Asset. The chapter on education will cover all the areas of self-education you need to incorporate into your life and the best sources of this self-education.

Money is another Life Asset. Every person at some point in their life had money or will continue to have money in some amount. The amount is not important. What you do with your money is what is important. Rich people are good at investing their money and making money work for them. Most people save money instead of investing it. The chapter on money will help you minimize your debt and maximize your current income. Getting out of debt is one of the best goals a person can have.

Health is the most important Life Asset in every person's life. Unlike time, we all don't get the same amount of good health. Some people have good health and some people may have bad health, but we all have some level of this asset. If you aren't healthy, you can't set goals and make the effort to change your life and become rich. Rich people guard and value their health. They want to be healthy so they can work hard to increase their net worth and income and have the time and energy to enjoy the fruits of their efforts. Without good health it is hard to change your life and become rich. Therefore, Health is a very important Life Asset.

One of the biggest differences that sets rich people apart from everyone else is that they understand what the six Life Assets are and are careful every day to get the most out of them. Most people are not aware of the concept of Life Assets. They have no idea that mindset, people, time, knowledge, money, and health are superpowers that can be used to change their lives. If guarded and leveraged on a regular basis, your Life Assets will make you rich, healthy, and happy. Most people do nothing intentionally day in and day out to use these Assets to change their lives for the better. If they only knew what they are missing.

I am a living example of what happens when a person works smart and hard over time bringing value to other people. Now that I leverage my six Life Assets, my health, happiness, knowledge, income, and net worth continue to grow every day. The remainder of the book will cover each Life Asset in detail. Harnessing the power of these Assets will be critical if you want to change your life and become rich.

ASSET #1: MINDSET

DEVELOP A SUCCESSFUL MINDSET

"Every next level of your life will demand a different you."
--Leonardo DiCaprio

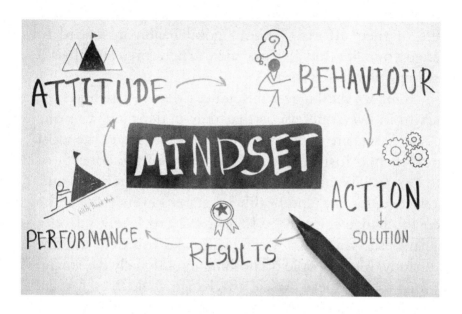

    The first Asset that we all have available to us is our *mindset*. As we continue talking about changing your life and changing your finances, we must back up and return to the source of everything: your mind. If you want to change your life and become rich, the very first thing you must change is your mindset. Until you truly believe in your heart and soul that you can be successful, that you can be wealthy, it will never happen. The change starts with your own thoughts.

The Law of Attraction

There are numerous Principles for Success or Laws of the Universe that exist and have been around for thousands of years. CEOs, leaders, politicians, scholars, poets, kings, and conquerors all use these principles and laws of the universe to help them obtain their goals, run companies, build cities, conquer lands, and acquire great wealth. One of the oldest and most powerful of these laws is the Law of Attraction.

The Law of Attraction is the belief that by focusing on positive or negative thoughts a person brings positive or negative experiences into their life. The belief is based on the idea that people and their thoughts are both made from "pure energy," and that through the process of "like energy attracting like energy" a person can improve their own health, wealth and personal relationships.

The Law of Attraction is the single biggest reason my life has improved in many ways, and my wealth and net worth continue to grow. My health, wealth, and happiness are more abundant now than ever before in my life. The only way to harness the power of the Law of Attraction is to develop and grow a positive mindset.

The Law of Attraction is not magic. It does not work instantly just because you become aware of it. It only works overtime if you live your life with the mindset of a positive wealthy person.

Your Why Statement

A Why statement defines the reasons you want to work hard and change your life. Knowing why you want something and staying focused on that reason will have a huge impact on your chances for success. You need a well-defined positive "Why" statement if you want to obtain financial freedom and build wealth.

Red Kettle Day

If you are passionate about what you will do for others as you grow your wealth and cash flow, it can drive you to unimaginable heights of success. Passion and desire are very powerful emotions. They can motivate a person to get outside of their comfort zone and work hard to accomplish a goal or a mission.

My friend Mike decided to enter a body transformation contest that was offered by the EAS supplement company. The winner of the contest would be the person who lost the most weight and had the lowest body fat percentage after a six-month time period. Mike weighed 240 pounds at the time he started his transformation. He was probably forty to sixty pounds overweight. Mike's typical weekend was sitting on a barstool at the bar my friends and I owned, drinking pints of Guinness beer. When Mike showed us the before and after photos of typical contestants and said he was going to win the contest, he was greeted with smiles and reservations about his chances. Over the next six months he trained, ate, dieted and ran like his life depended on it. He was obsessed with making a tremendous change and winning the contest.

Mike's transformation was miraculous to say the least. He lost sixty pounds, his body fat was in the single digit range and he was ripped like a competitive bodybuilder. Mike didn't win the contest, but he was a runner-up in his weight category nationally and won free supplements for a year. I will never forget his transformation. Mike's "Why" statement was to turn his life around, become the healthiest person possible and win the EAS supplement contest. His transformation is a testament to what is possible when a person has a very positive Why and is passionate to fulfill that Why.

A positive Why statement that benefits others is also important because bringing value to other people is the foundation of acquiring great wealth. One of my all-time favorite self-improvement gurus, Earl Nightingale said it best: "*Your income is directly proportional to the value you bring to other people.*" Another favorite self-improvement guru of mine, Zig Ziglar, has a famous statement: "*You can have anything you want in life if you help enough other people get what they want out of life.*"

One day I was asked by a real estate client why I try to help people so much and why I am always trying to pay it forward. Without even thinking I said to my client: "*The more people I help, the better my life gets!*" I think that statement sums it up.

Below are examples of some powerful and positive Why statements that a person can have:

- "To keep my family safe, secure, and give them all the important things life has to offer."
- "To help rejuvenate and remove blight from an inner-city neighborhood."
- "To find a cure for cancer."
- "To invent a portable water desalination system."
- "To improve aquaculture systems."

- "To start and own my dream company."
- "To start a company that responsibly competes in an industry or market segment."
- "To help a local charity purchase a building for their operations."
- "To pay for a vacation for my parents to visit their homeland."

Visualization

Another way to become obsessed about money is to see, hear, and touch the things that acquiring money will allow you to accomplish, purchase, and create. I call this the *"See it, touch it habit."* If you look at the object of your desire often enough, you will eventually start taking steps to acquire it.

I've heard many success and wealth building gurus say that if you want a big house you should drive through the neighborhoods where those homes are as often as possible. If you want an expensive car, then drive around those car lots and see your dream car. I learned the power of this lesson on my own very early in life.

When I was ten years old, I wanted a bicycle in the worst way. At that point in my life I had never owned a bike. My parents did not have the extra money to buy me a bike. When my friends rode their bikes down to the baseball fields, I would run alongside of them to keep up. Growing up, money was very tight in our household and always a subject that caused arguments.

At that time, I was hanging out with a couple kids who were not a good influence on me. They got into shoplifting and dared me to do it. Unfortunately, I decided to take them up on their dare and I stole a bunch of items from the local drugstore. This was my first lesson in life about surrounding myself with the wrong people. I will talk more in detail about this concept later in the book, when we cover the Life Asset of People.

I shared the secret details about my shoplifting adventures with my brother who promptly ran to my parents and told them. My mother spanked me and when my father got home, he spanked me even worse. Then I was grounded after school for three months. I also had to go to the drugstore owner and admit what I had done. My parents then made me work for free at the drugstore after school until my wages paid back all the merchandise I stole.

Unfortunately for me, my parents were not done punishing me. It was a couple of weeks before Christmas. I didn't know it, but my parents bought me my first bike as a Christmas present. When they found out I was shoplifting they brought the bike into the house, showed it to me, and told me as part of my punishment I would not receive the bike on Christmas day. They kept their word and returned the bike to the store where they purchased it. I don't think you could break a kid's heart more than that. All the other kids in the neighborhood had bikes except for me. I was crushed. The entire next summer I ran alongside my friends as they rode their bikes to the baseball field to play baseball or I would tell them I would catch up to them later while I walked.

I had to solve this transportation problem as soon as possible. There was a Schwinn bike shop four blocks from my house. I spent most of that summer visiting that bike shop to stare at the bikes I wished I owned. Every day, I fixed my gaze on the most incredible 10-speed bike. The bike was $120 and the most expensive bike in the shop. I was in love with that bright yellow Schwinn ten-speed bike. The more I looked at that bike the more obsessed I became with acquiring it. It would be the best bike in the entire neighborhood and all my friends would be jealous. If I could get that bike, I would instantly surpass them in the kid transportation pecking order. I had one big problem. I was a 10-year-old with no money!

A day didn't go by that I didn't stop at the bike shop to gawk at that bike. I racked my brain for ways to get money because the image of that bike was driving me crazy.

Fortunately for me, my cousin Tim was delivering newspapers at the time and he asked me to help him out. I helped him organize the papers and insert the ad sections. I went with him on his route and helped him deliver the papers to his customer's doorsteps. After a few weeks I knew I could handle delivering papers. The irony was you needed a bike to carry and efficiently deliver the papers— and obviously, I had no bike. After some negotiating and debating I convinced my parents to let me get a small paper route. I used an old metal wagon to load and transport my papers and I was in business.

After the first two weeks of delivering newspapers I received my first $5 paycheck. I ran over to the Schwinn bike shop and made my first payment on the ten-speed Schwinn bike. When I was growing up you could put a retail item on what was called layaway. The store owner would hold the merchandise you wanted in their stock room until you made all the payments. We didn't have credit cards back then—so, for me, this was a way to make sure I was steadily getting closer to my goal of owning that bike.

After making each payment, I would stay at the shop for another thirty minutes and stare at that beautiful bike. I couldn't take my eyes off it. Luckily, the store owner was very accommodating and let me hang out to admire the object of my desire.

After a few months of making layaway payments, I did some math and realized it was going to take me way too long to purchase this bike. I asked the newspaper delivery manager for more paper routes, but none were available. Then one day the largest route became available. When the manager asked me if I wanted it, I jumped all over it. Now I was rocking and rolling. I was making $18 every two weeks and throwing every penny I could at getting that bike.

Finally, the day came when I had the money to make the final payment. I can't explain how excited I was as I finished my paper route that day so I could get to the bike shop as fast as possible. When the shop owner brought the bike out to me, he asked for the attention of all the employees and the customers in the store. He congratulated me in front of everyone, told them all how dedicated I was for making all the payments, and how long it took for me to get the bike. I will never forget how proud I was that day.

Now was the moment I had been waiting for over a year: my first ride through the neighborhood on the most expensive and glorious bike in the entire block. I took my time and rode as slowly as I could up and down the block until all my friends saw me. They couldn't believe it. They all ran up to me asking me all kinds of questions and asking if they could take it for a ride. Of course, the answer was no. I was *"The Man!"* Victory was mine.

Seeing that bike every day and imagining what it was going to be like when I finally owned it made me take extreme action to achieve that goal. The moral of the story is if you constantly remind yourself you can do it and visualize yourself succeeding and obtaining your goal, it will happen. If you really want it, truly believe you can succeed, and consistently visualize the outcome you will succeed.

This story illustrates the power of visualization. If delivering newspapers had not been an option, I would have found another way to get the money. Looking at that bike every day drove me to acquire it by every means possible.

Looking at magazine pictures of places you want to visit, watching videos of things you want to accomplish, following successful people online who have started the business you want to start is a fantastic way to get motivated. For years I would look at fly fishing magazines to see the awesome photos of trophy fish being caught in exotic far away locations. Now I take those trips every year. I went to Alaska for a week of fishing in August 2015. It was an epic trip. I went to Kiritimati island in the South Pacific in February of 2018 for some of the world's

Fishing on Christmas Island and in Alaska

best bone fishing. Whenever you get a free hour, go to a bookstore and spend some time looking at magazine photos of the things you want from life like surfing, fishing trips, real estate, travel destinations, etc.

My wife and I frequently vacation in Rehoboth Beach, Delaware. On the drive from Erie to Rehoboth we pass through Lancaster, PA. I have always wanted to own a modern cash flow producing self-storage facility. One of the greatest indoor climate-controlled facilities is in Lancaster, PA. Every time we take the trip to Rehoboth, we get off at the Lancaster exit where Supreme Self-storage is located. I go to the property and get out and walk around the building. I love seeing this investment property. I'll even go inside and walk around the interior and take photos if the door is open. It is the self-storage facility of my dreams, and I know some day I will own one like it.

Some examples of the visualization habit include:

- Drive by the investment property you want to own.
- Tour Open Houses of the homes you want to live in.
- Visiting the business you want to be in.

- Looking at magazines with photos of the goals you want to reach.
- Watching YouTube videos or TV shows that show you the objects of your desire.

The *"See it, touch it habit"* has paid huge dividends for me. It is one of the best visualization techniques to get you motivated so you can live the life of your dreams.

Vision Boards

A vision board is another great visualization technique. It is a graphical representation of your dreams, goals, ideas, passions, and Why statements. It is a collection of photos, drawings, text, and images that you can use to remind yourself of what you are working for. Looking at images of your goals and dreams will stimulate and strengthen your thoughts. It creates more positive energy which helps trigger the law of attraction in your life.

Hang your vision board on a wall that you walk past frequently—this could be in your kitchen, bedroom, or office. This is a great way to view your visual goals and dreams every day.

Start by writing your Why Statement at the very top of your vision board. It might read something like this: "*I want to get out of debt and obtain financial freedom so I can start a community college that teaches under-privileged residents how to work in the building trades.*"

Then write down some words or phrases that describe your goals and dreams. These could be phrases like: Financial Freedom; Vacation Home; Debt-Free; Community College; or even Mercedes-Benz. Make sure these words are bold and in large text so you can read them from a distance.

Next, add photos of your loved ones or the people whose lives you want to change, when you make your dreams a reality. Last of all, add photos of what you want to obtain from life. By looking at your vision board on a regular basis, you will keep the things you want to have, do, or be at the front of your consciousness. It will not be long before your wishes start coming true.

Remember to hang your vision board someplace you will see it several times a day. Make a point of looking at it when you first get up in the morning and before you go to bed at night.

Example Vision Boards

"I want to work doing what I want, when I want, and where I want."

"I want to get out of debt and obtain financial freedom so I can start a community college that teaches under-privileged residents how to work in the building trades."

"I want to take my parents on a vacation to their homeland so they can see all the relatives they have not visited in decades."

Financial Freedom
Vacation Home
Debt-Free
Mercedes-Benz
Trip to Italy
Non-profit free Trade school for under-privileged residents

Meditation

More and more successful wealthy entrepreneurs are realizing the value of regular meditation. Meditation helps reduce stress and keep you focused on what is important. It helps you to not worry about the past or too far out in the future. Meditation before you go to bed will calm you down, reduce anxiety and help you fall asleep at night. It is good for your physical and mental health. Meditation about positive events, gratitude and affirmations, creates positive energy which triggers the Law of Attraction. I highly recommend ten to fifteen minutes of meditation every day.

A technique I use to involve my subconscious mind and leverage visualization is a six-step meditation thought process right before I go to sleep at night. After I am lying in bed with all the lights out, and I am preparing to fall asleep I close my eyes and perform the following five thought processes.

First, I use controlled breathing to help to me reduce any stress or anxiety that has accumulated during the day. Controlled breathing is a great way to decompress after a long day of work and play. I take ten deep slow controlled breaths. I recite in my mind as I breath in, the words "Calm in." I recite in my mind as I breath out, the words "Worry out." Controlled breathing helps settle me down and prepare me for sleep.

Second, I use the concept of gratitude to review all the wonderful things in my life I am thankful for. Even the comfortable bed I am laying in. The food I ate that day. The love I gave and received from family and friends. I express my gratitude for the day for all the simple things we all sometimes take for granted.

Third, I do what I call my confession. I apologize for anything I did that day that was inconsiderate, possibly made another person feel bad or generated any negative energy in my mind and body. The Law of Attraction only works if you are generating positive energy. This confession allows me to generate more positive energy and remove any negative energy from the day. We are all human and we make mistakes. We all do things that might not be nice. If I cut someone off in traffic or looked at another person and made a judgmental thought in my mind, it is not nice, and it generates negative energy. I ask for forgiveness for anything that was mean or not nice. I always feel better after I spend a minute reviewing what I could have done better that day.

Fourth, I read my Why statement in my mind to remind myself why I am trying to be the best person I can be and why I want to obtain financial success.

"I want to acquire and maintain financial success so I can take care of my family in any situation life presents."

"I want to acquire and maintain financial success so I can help other people change their lives, realize their goals and enjoy financial freedom."

"I want to acquire and maintain financial success so I no longer need a job and can work where I want, when I want, doing what I love."

Fifth, I recite my goals with intention, that will support my Why statement.

"I will own fifty income producing rental properties."

"My real estate brokerage will have a team of 30

successful real estate agents."

"I will own a profitable education business based on book sales, seminars and paid speaking engagements."

Last, and most importantly, I imagine in my mind how I am already living the life of my dreams. One of my goals is to spend an entire summer in Rehoboth Beach Delaware writing my next book. Rehoboth Beach is a small-town right on the ocean in Delaware. Rehoboth Avenue leads down to the board walk on the ocean, and I enjoy spending time in the cafes and eateries.

In my mind I imagine sitting in the outdoor seating at The Mill coffee shop or one of the great Crepe shops. The sun is shining, and the air is warm. I'm wearing a T-shirt, shorts and flip flops. I already hit the gym that morning and had a great breakfast. I can smell the salt air from the ocean, and someone walks buy and smells like suntan lotion. My coffee tastes awesome.

The Money Playbook

I want to introduce you to a brilliant tool for changing your life and acquiring anything you want. This method, a true secret weapon in your arsenal of life-changing techniques, has helped me manifest and acquire all forms of happiness, money, health, personal achievement, and investment assets. This secret weapon I invented is called the Money Playbook.

If you want to build a house, you need tools and a blueprint. If you want to start a company, you need a business plan, systems, and processes. If you want to find buried treasure, you need the treasure map. In the same way, if you want to change your life and become rich, you will need tools, systems, plans, and maps. The Money Playbook is all those things and more. It has been the blueprint for change for me and can be for you.

The photo on the next page is the original version of my first Money Playbook. On the surface the Money Playbook looks like an ordinary composition notebook.

What makes my Money Playbook so powerful is what is on the inside. The money playbook is made up of four sections:

1. Your Why Statement.
2. The Cash Flow Creed.
3. The Success Manifesto.
4. Your daily ritual of declarations, motivations, gratitude statements, and goals.

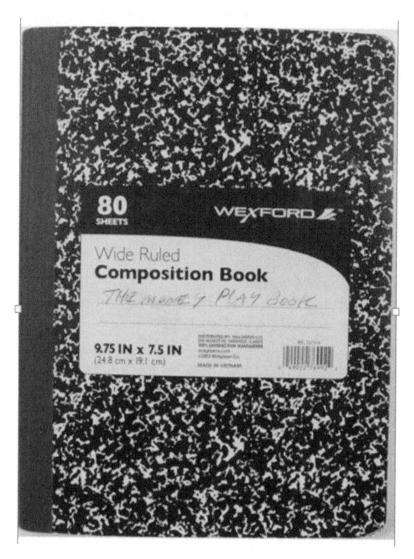

If you want to change your life and become rich, then it is time for you to create your own Money Playbook. The Money Playbook is your blueprint for success. You will use the Money Playbook daily to generate positive energy, motivation, and massive change. This tool will help you manifest the life you want and deserve.

The Money Playbook is a powerful system to help you harness the power of the Law of Attraction and put it to work for you. The Money Playbook is a structured easy-to-use tool that generates and attracts the universe's positive energy. Initially it might seem too easy that just writing and reading what you want out of life will bring those things to you. All I can tell you is it works, and it works well. I have used the Money Playbook and the Law of Attraction for years to create an abundant and happy life. If you want to change your life and become rich you must start using your Money Playbook immediately.

How to Use the Money Playbook

Purchase a composition-style notebook like the one in the previous photo. I like the composition-style notebook because it's light, small, thin, and easy to carry around. The lines are the right size and the pages don't rip out over time. Do not use computer software or a cell phone app to take the place of this notebook. It's important to physically hand write the words into the Playbook since writing is a process that affects your subconscious mind.

On the very first page of the Money Playbook, write your Why statements. Some examples might be:

- I want to become financially free so I can provide a better life for my family and help people less fortunate than me.
- I want to send my children to college.
- I want to be able to afford to help my parents retire.
  Your Why statements are the very first thing you will

read out loud when you get up in the morning and before you go to bed at night. As you read each statement try to visualize in your mind what your life will be like when you accomplish the goals stated in your Why statements.

Next you will write down the Cash Flow Creed. The Webster's dictionary definition for Creed is: *A set of fundamental beliefs, a guiding principle.*

Cash Flow Creed

This creed will outline your fundamental beliefs about money in your life. It will be made up of statements you want to remind yourself of daily, so they become your set of beliefs. I would suggest that you write down the following ten statements that form the Cash Flow Creed, on the second page of your Money Playbook. Make sure you have some space between each statement, so they will be easy to read.

1. My life is full of abundance and limitless opportunity.
2. I value, protect and leverage my six Life Assets.
3. I deserve all the prosperity and abundance life has to offer.
4. I have the mindset of a rich person.
5. Money loves me and wants to be with me because I treat it with care and do good things with it.
6. Money flows to me constantly. It comes to me easily and effortlessly.
7. Cash flow producing assets are all around me.
8. Every day my wealth and income are increasing.
9. I am open and receptive to increased income and all financial opportunity.
10. I will use my wealth and income to help people less fortunate than me.

The Cash Flow Creed is the second thing you will read out loud when you get up in the morning and before you go to bed at night. As you read each statement, try to visualize in your mind what the words mean to you and how your life will look with these new beliefs.

On the third page of your Money Playbook you will write down the Success Manifesto. The Webster dictionary definition for Manifesto is: *A written statement declaring publicly the intentions, motives or views of its issuer.*

This manifesto will specify who you are as a person and what you want your dream life to look like. When you read it to yourself each day, you'll be reminded of what's truly important to you. My Success Manifesto looks like this:

1. My thoughts, beliefs and attitude will determine my future.
2. I am completely responsible for where I am in life today.
3. I have the power, strength and knowledge to change any part of my life.
4. It doesn't matter how much money I have now or what my current education level is, I can achieve any goal I desire.
5. I am powerful, successful and smart. There is no limit to what I can accomplish in my life.
6. My life is a result of who I am today. If I want to change my life, then I must change me.
7. There is no such thing as getting rich quick. All my goals and dreams will require working smart and hard over time.
8. Now is the best time for me to set my goals and start changing my life.
9. Nobody can stop me from reaching my goals and dreams.
10. Nothing is owed to me by another person or the universe. If I want change, I must earn it.
11. I deserve and will have great health, increased income and happiness for me and my family.

The Success Manifesto is the third thing you will read out loud when you get up in the morning and before you go to bed at night. You will read the Success Manifesto right after you read the Cash Flow Creed. Reading the Success Manifesto out loud every day will cement in your mind these beliefs. These are the beliefs of rich people and if you want to change your life and become rich then you must truly subscribe to these beliefs. As you read each statement out loud in the Success Manifesto, try to visualize in your mind what the words mean. Read each statement twice if it helps.

Gratitudes

The fourth process I do every day in my Money Playbook is to write several declarations, motivations, gratitude statements, and goals. The Money Playbook is the place to write down what you want out of life, recognize all the wonderful things about yourself, and list what you are thankful for. Doing this daily is guaranteed to change your beliefs, attitude, and entire outlook on life.

Why Read Out Loud

Reading out loud significantly increases the impact of the content of your Money Playbook. Studies show that when we say something out loud, we increase how much we remember. Memory retention is stronger than reading silently to ourselves. Also, research shows that talking to yourself out loud can help motivate you to take more action towards your goals. It has been proven that athletes that mutter positive motivational affirmations out loud to themselves during competition perform better than athletes who stay silent.

In the upcoming chapters, you'll be able to generate plenty of statements for your own Money Playbook. Below is an example of the declarations, motivations, gratitude statements, and goals that I write in the Money Playbook each day:

DECLARATIONS
I am a happy husband.
I am smart and successful.
I am a great real estate broker.
I am strong, confident and happy.
I have the mindset of a rich person.

MOTIVATIONS
I must get out of debt.
I must finish my college degree.
I must prosper and reinvent myself.
I must learn to bring more value to other people.

GRATITUDE STATEMENTS
I love my family.

I love my dogs.
I love money.
I love real estate.

GOALS
I will finish my book this year.
I will buy ten more rental units.
I will work out three times a week.
I will attend one seminar every year.

All this writing and reading out loud creates your rituals and builds a strong mindset. Rituals are very powerful. They are a critical process for any person who wants to change their life and become rich. The most successful people in the world develop a strong and positive mindset using rituals and a daily practice like the Money Playbook.

A major step to becoming rich is to significantly increase your expectations for life. You owe it to yourself and your family to succeed. This can only be done if you desire to be rich and you expect it. You must settle for nothing less than true financial freedom. If you want more from yourself then expect more from yourself. If you want more out of life, then expect more out of life. If you want more money, then expect more money.

If you don't have any expectations for yourself, then life will push you around. What if you didn't have any expectations for your kids? How would they turn out? What if they knew you didn't expect them to behave, do their homework, brush their teeth and go to bed on time? They would be in trouble all the time and get kicked out of school. What if your boss had no expectations of you? You would show up late and do very little work. When we have expectations of ourselves, we perform better. It is the same for changing your life and becoming rich. If you don't expect it, then it won't happen. If you expect it, then it will happen.

Thoughts happen. If your thoughts are focused on higher expectations, then this is what will happen. If you want more out of life, then you must expect more out of life.

Believe me when I tell you that you deserve to have a successful and happy life just as much as any person on this planet. You deserve to be rich and successful. You are worthy of everything life has to offer. If you are going to realize your happiness and wealth potential, you must believe you deserve it and are worthy.

ACCEPT THESE BELIEFS

If you want to change your life and become rich, the first thing you must change are your belief systems. Our belief systems are the foundation for where we are in life. Our health, happiness, accomplishments, and wealth are all controlled by our beliefs. Our belief systems shape our mindset and our mindset controls our day-to-day actions and decisions. What we believe causes us to *think* and *act*, both of which are activities that create our reality.

Albert Einstein is credited with saying; *"The definition of insanity is doing the same thing over and over and expecting different results."* If you are not rich and you want to become rich, then you must change everything about yourself, especially your beliefs. Everything you have done, learned, thought, or believed needs to change. You must reevaluate all that you eat and drink, everything you listen to, and the kinds of people you hang around. If you can change your mindset and your beliefs, then you have the power to change all other aspects of your life.

If you want to revolutionize your life and realize your dreams, then it's important to start with these three central concepts:

1. You must know what you want and be passionate about acquiring it.
2. You need to put in the effort to acquire the knowledge needed to pursue your passion.
3. You need the confidence to implement this knowledge and take the risks.

The third item in the list above is the most important. Most people never act and go after what they want in life because they don't truly believe they can be successful. They lack the confidence and positive attitude they need to take the first step toward changing anything. They stay the same rather than risk anything. Most people live inside their comfort zone for their entire lives. The funny thing is, I'll hear people complain about how they wish they were living a different life. They might long to be doing something else for a living. But as soon as you start encouraging them to pursue that passion, they come up with every excuse in the book for why they can't. Their beliefs are truly holding them back, not their ability. They simply believe all the wrong things about themselves and the world around them.

I go on fly-fishing trips every few years with a close friend of mine, an avid fly fisherman who I met while we were both engineers outside of Boston. He's mentioned more than once that he's miserable working as an engineer and would rather follow his dream of owning a fly-fishing lodge. My friend is very smart, likable, and good at relating to other people. He has a vast knowledge of fly-fishing techniques and even makes his own fly rods and flies. He has all the skills needed to be successful at owning a lodge or B&B for anglers. But every time we talk about him leaving the engineering profession to pursue his dream, he begins listing the reasons it would never work. He finally admitted to me that he lacks confidence and doesn't believe he could be successful at owning his own business.

When I examine my upbringing, I remember many instances when my father didn't encourage me to pursue my dreams. Don't get me wrong—he was a hardworking person and never put his own needs before his family. But he was also very negative and would routinely be the first person to doubt me or tell me I was making the wrong choice when I tried to go out of my comfort zone. No matter what I did around the house, he said I didn't do it right. He never trusted anyone, and he blamed everyone for where he was in life.

Based on my relationship with my father, I should be a complete failure. In fact, if you look at the first half of my life, I *was* a complete failure. I failed in dating relationships, I flunked out of college, I couldn't keep my business ventures from flopping, and I was fired from my first job as an engineer. I even totaled the first four cars I owned! I had a very defensive personality and a negative view of everything.

So, how did I change my life from failure to fortune? Was it that the beliefs were there all along, but I didn't know how to use them, or did I need to completely change my belief systems? For me, it was a bit of both. Ever since I was a kid, I always knew that I could be successful and rich. Because I held this belief, I never gave up trying, even when life was difficult, and I found myself failing time and time again. I made a ton of mistakes but used trial and error to learn, all the while remembering that I could—and would—succeed. That single belief—that I knew I could do it—empowered me. As life went on, I replaced many negative beliefs with powerful beliefs along the way that helped shape my prosperity.

When I talk about changing your beliefs, I'm not referring to any religious or political perspective but rather the most basic emotional and logical ways you process information. Just as you take in food through your mouth to begin the digestion process, you also absorb 'food' for your mind through your eyes and ears. I will use the term 'Mind Food' to refer to this flow of information. When Mind Food enters your body, your belief systems determine how you process and react to it. Your belief systems control your decision making. If you make positive decisions, then positive things will grow in your life. If you make negative decisions, then negative things will grow in your life. If you believe you can be successful at pursuing your dreams, then you will succeed. If you don't think you are smart enough to succeed, then you won't. It's really that simple.

There are two types of Mind Food: Voluntary Mind Food and Involuntary Mind Food. Voluntary Mind Food is what you choose to watch, read, and listen to. We can choose these things. We have the free will to decide what we read and view, as well as the kinds of people we associate with and what we talk about when we're together with them.

Involuntary Mind Food includes all those inputs you can't control. You might witness a car accident or see a person trip and fall. You drive down the road and when you look out the window you see a building or a corn field. You engage in conversation with people, but you can't regulate what they talk about. There are numerous situations where we have no control over what we see and hear.

What you do have control over is your intake of Voluntary Mind Food as well as how you react to both the Voluntary and Involuntary Mind Food.

Have you ever heard the saying *garbage in equals garbage out*? This is a concept common to computer science and mathematics: the quality of output is determined by the quality of the input. For example, if a mathematical equation is improperly stated, the answer is unlikely to be correct. You can also use this saying to describe the food you eat. If you have a terrible diet of junk food, sugar, and salt, you will likely suffer from a lack of energy, mood changes, and possible health problems.

Garbage in equals garbage out also applies to what you consume with your eyes and ears. Another important aspect to becoming rich is seeking out positive Voluntary Mind Food so that you are better equipped to handle the Involuntary Mind Food that sneaks its way into your life. Later in this book, I'll talk more about how to focus on bringing good quality Mind Food into your life.

What's important to understand right now is that your belief systems impact how you choose your Voluntary Mind Food and how you handle the Involuntary Mind Food. Your belief systems and your Mind Food work in concert. There is no way you can become rich without the belief systems of rich people and a flow of Voluntary Mind Food that empowers your ability to change and grow.

As I was learning how to become successful, I found that I had to change many negative beliefs in my life that were holding me back in significant ways. I had to embrace a completely new set of beliefs in order to really change my life for the better. These beliefs are non-negotiable in the pursuit of any kind of tremendous change. What follows is a list of the beliefs you must embrace and put into practice if you want to bring success and wealth into your own life.

BELIEF #1: Whatever you believe is what will happen.

"We become what we think about."
— Earl Nightingale

Something you need to get your arms around right now is the fact that what you believe is what will happen. I don't have the answer as to why this is true, but I know the universe will give you what you believe will happen. If you think good things will happen to you, then good things are what you get. If you think negative things will happen to you, then negative things are what you get. This is one of the best examples of the Law of Attraction. It is undeniable and inescapable. You can't fight it, change it, or defeat it. If you choose to ignore this belief, your life will stay the same and you will never have any choice over what happens to you. Whatever your financial, happiness, and health status is today, it has been formed by your beliefs. If you accept and think about any belief concept, this is the most critical of all beliefs to accept and be conscious of every day for the rest of your life. Without this belief, you will never succeed at anything in life. This belief is the key to changing your life and achieving success in any endeavor.

In 2006, the book titled *The Secret* was published. It was a tremendous success, though it was really nothing new. It was based on the centuries old Law of Attraction that numerous scholars, historians, and leaders were aware of long ago. Self-improvement gurus like Jim Rohn, Earl Nightingale, and Zig Ziglar spoke about this law way before The Secret was ever written.

The Law of Attraction is the belief that by focusing on positive or negative thoughts, a person brings positive or negative experiences into their life. The belief is based on the idea that people and their thoughts are both made from "pure energy," and that through the process of "like energy attracting like energy" a person can improve their own health, wealth and personal relationships.

Notice how the word **"belief"** is in the beginning of this description. Many self-improvement writers and speakers use the law to teach people how to transform their wealth, health, and personal relationships.

I love the often-told story of the two boys who were ice skating on a frozen pond. One of the boys fell through the ice and got trapped underneath. His friend started to frantically punch the ice but couldn't get through to save his friend. Out of desperation, he climbed a tree, broke off a large branch, and used it to smash the ice.

Eventually, the boy was able to break through and pulled his friend out of the freezing water. Shortly thereafter, emergency services arrived at the scene. They were amazed and expressed wonder at how such a little boy was able to break off such a large branch, smash the inches-thick ice, and single-handedly pull his little friend out. As they shared their amazement, an old man walked up to them and answered their question. He told them: "The boy was able to do it because there was no one there who told him he couldn't."

During my days working as a software developer at an electronics manufacturer, I often walked past a poster out on the shop floor that read: *"Whether you think you can, or you think you can't, either way you are right."* This quote from Henry Ford is one of my favorites as it reminds us that our thoughts determine our future.

I'd like to share another story that illustrates the power of a positive attitude. A friend of mine, who was involved with a multi-level marketing sales company, kept asking me to attend one of his sales meetings. He wanted me to hear how great the company was to try to recruit me to his sales force. I wasn't all that interested in the opportunity until he mentioned that the number one salesperson in the company would be there to speak. I agreed to attend only to hear this salesperson, hoping I'd learn something useful for my own career. The speaker's main quote was *"Thoughts happen."*

His story intrigued me. He'd wanted to be one of the best salespeople at his company so that he could buy all those material possessions that reflected his success and helped him live a comfortable life. He wanted to drive an expensive car and live in a big house. To that end, he resolved to drive past the car lot every day on his way home, so he could see the expensive car he would someday own. Every day on his way to work, he took a detour through a neighborhood of luxury homes. Seeing the objects of his desire every single day kept him motivated and held the rewards in his mind constantly. Each day he went to work and geared his actions toward achieving those things he wanted. Within three years, he owned both the house and the car of his dreams.

Another way to change your beliefs is to start acting like the person you want to become. When I became a real estate agent I wanted to be as successful as the senior agent in my office and the owner of the entire real estate brokerage. These guys wore suits and ties every day to work. I went to the local men's clothing store and purchased new dress shirts, ties, and sport coats so I could act like and be perceived as successful as these real estate gurus.

I once made a list of the names of the most successful people in the world. *Bill Gates, Jeff Bezos, Mark Zuckerberg, Joe Herbert, and Warren Buffett.* That's right, *Joe Herbert* was on that list! I taped the list to my bathroom mirror, so I could see it every day. I wanted to perceive myself in the same light as these billionaires. I wanted to believe it could happen—that I could be the success I wanted to be.

If you want to get somewhere in life, you need to start acting like the person you want to become. You must accept the fact that your beliefs are controlling your life.

BELIEF #2: You must accept complete responsibility for where you are today.

"If you could kick the person in the pants responsible for most of your trouble, you wouldn't sit for a month."
—Theodore Roosevelt

Second in the list of beliefs you must embrace in order to have the right mindset for success is this: only you are responsible for your life. It's imperative that you accept complete responsibility for where you are today. Every aspect of your life—the house you live in, your credit score, your health, how much money you earn, your debt, how you feel, how you look, your education level, what you do for a living, and who you share your days with—is entirely up to you.

If you're not satisfied with where you are today, it really isn't the fault of your parents, the government, or your employer. Most of all stop blaming this thing called life. Life has not been unfair to you. Life has not deprived you of luck. Life will give you what you give life. It is that simple. Blaming is an unproductive act that serves no one, especially not yourself. Only once you stop the blame game, will you be able to create the mental space to begin building the life of your dreams.

If you make bad choices and surround yourself with negative people, then life will give you pain and suffering. If you make good choices—like thinking positively, taking care of your mind and body, and educating yourself—then life will gift you with beautiful things. Stop complaining about how you can't catch a break and how your ship hasn't come in. You are where you are right now because of the choices you have made. Until you accept complete responsibility for your life, you will never be able to change any part of it.

BELIEF #3: You are in complete control of your future.

"No one saves us but ourselves. No one can, and no one may. We ourselves must walk the path."
— Buddha

It doesn't matter where you are in life at this moment. You can be the type of person to sleep in or sit on the couch and watch Netflix all day—or you can get out of bed early and start changing your life. You have all the power and control, and nobody is going to make those choices and decisions for you.

You, and only you, are responsible for changing your own future. Only you can effectively make the necessary changes to improve your life. There is nothing and nobody in this world that is holding you back except you. You are the only person who can decide what happens tomorrow.

Once you've accepted that you and your choices are why you are where you are in life, then you are responsible for changing things to make your life better. You are the only person who can decide what happens tomorrow. Don't wait for your 'break.' You catch a cold or a ball— you don't catch a break.

In my experience, I've heard people make excuses for why they don't feel their life is going that well. Some of the most common excuses used by people who are too afraid to take control of their lives are:

1. I wasn't born with a silver spoon in my mouth.
2. I'm cursed, I can't catch a break, and I have the worst luck.
3. I'm too nice, and the last time I tried that I got screwed. No thanks.

4. You don't know what I am dealing with right now.
5. I don't have the time.
6. I'm not smart enough.
7. I'm too old now or I'm too young to start.
8. Now isn't a good time. As soon as some event happens or passes by then I will start.
9. I can't afford it.
10. I'm afraid what people will think about my goals.

The truth is every single person on this earth has the chance to take their life to the next level. Lasting positive change is possible for everyone who is willing to embrace the right mindset. The world-famous German-born diarist and World War II Holocaust victim Anne Frank wrote: *"The final forming of a person's character lies in their own hands."* Start becoming rich right now by accepting complete responsibility for what happens to you and the rest of your life.

BELIEF #4: It doesn't matter who you are or where you came from.

"You can influence, direct, and control your own environment. You can make your life what you want it to be."
— Napoleon Hill

Every person has the potential to change their life for the better. It doesn't matter where you are financially, educationally, socially, emotionally, or even geographically. Success doesn't care where you come from or whether your family's name is impressive. Success does not care if you flunked out of high school or if you have a college degree. Success only cares that you are looking for it, that you want it worse than your next breath, and that you're willing to work for it. Success, wealth, and happiness are free and available to all of us. The belief systems, principles for success, and wealth-building knowledge to obtain anything you want in life are free—and they work for every person who will apply them.

If you weren't born with that silver spoon in your mouth, that's fine. It only means you must make enough changes that you can afford to buy your own silver spoon! For you, this might mean you need to get yourself out of debt or obtain more education. Maybe you want to land that perfect job or start your own business. Whatever your dream of success, it's there waiting for you to manifest it. Stop letting other people set your bar for you—rip that bar out of their hands and set it as high as you want!

Characteristics like age, race, ethnicity, or gender have no bearing on a person's potential for success or wealth-building. Nor do things like sexual orientation, family status, or where your luck lies right now in terms of income or employment or net worth. Yes, you probably have made mistakes in the past. But you can still do whatever you want to do in this world if you have the will to try.

I'm sharing these belief systems with you now because I truly believe they'll help you find success. If you apply the principles, then money will follow you. It will gravitate toward you because you will think, act, and talk like a rich person. All the money you need to be successful has already been printed and is available to you. The fact that it's not in your possession right now… well, that's only a minor factor. It won't determine whether you obtain success and wealth.

I will always use myself as a notable example of what can be accomplished with the right mindset and working smart and hard over time to bring value to other people. My parents had no money and worked minimum wage jobs their entire life. My father did not finish high school and my mother had only a high school education. I grew up across the street from a bar and two blocks from the railroad tracks. I was a bad student all through grade school, high school, and college. I flunked out of college after one year and made every relationship, money, education, and job mistake a person could make.

My life turned around completely when I discovered the Law of Attraction and changed my belief systems. My health, happiness, and wealth have been growing ever since. My life is proof you can start with nothing and become very successful when you learn to think like a rich person.

Several of my close friends started out in humble circumstances but are now multi-millionaires. These guys started with no money in their pockets but somehow became wealthy. Their parents were middle-class workers. The one thing they all have in common is they worked smart and hard over time, while, of course, bringing value to other people.

A good friend of mine went to prison for selling drugs. When he was released, he went on to receive two college degrees, start several businesses, become a social entrepreneur, and earn much well-deserved regard in his community. I have a ton of respect for him. He is a true success story. He proves the belief that it does not matter where you are in life right now. You can change your life and become rich if you are willing to take the first step and do the right things.

Another friend I grew up with in my neighborhood got his high school degree and then completed a four-year enlistment in the army. His family wasn't wealthy and didn't hand him a huge inheritance. Yet he was able to begin a thriving business through sheer force of his will. He began washing cars for a living and then got his car dealership license. Fast forward 20 years and he is now a multi-millionaire who owns several lucrative dealerships, a profitable stock portfolio, and numerous income-producing real estate properties. He achieved all of this by believing he would succeed, not caring where he was from, and working smart and hard over time bringing value to other people.

BELIEF #5: Your potential is limitless.

"I want to challenge you today to get out of your comfort zone. You have so much incredible potential on the inside. God has put gifts and talents in you that you probably don't know anything about."
— Joel Osteen

You can accomplish anything you want in life. You possess the power to change and become anything you want to become. You can design and manifest any life you desire for yourself. It doesn't matter where you are in life right now or where you come from. Your current financial, mental, social, or geographic situation does not matter.

Studies have shown that the richest billionaires do not have a college degree. In fact, studies have shown that a person's education level, IQ, and past school grades had no bearing on the outcome of their level of success. You will discover as you go forward on your journey for success that your level of desire and amount of effort you put in are the most critical factors. Your college degree, IQ, and resume have little or no bearing on whether you will be successful or not.

The movie *Facing the Giants*, which is about an underdog high school football team, is an awesome example of the human will to succeed and how we are all capable of incredible accomplishments.

In the famous *Death Crawl scene*, the head football coach blindfolds one of his players and asks him to crawl on his hands and feet across the playing field from the goal line to the 50-yard line, with another player riding on his back. Since a bandana covers his eyes, the player can't tell how close he is to the 50-yard line. Before long, the kid is complaining to the coach that he's exhausted. The coach gets down in the boy's face and yells encouragement, screaming, "Don't quit 'til you got nothin' left!" This tough love tactic encourages the high school boy to give his very best and to keep driving until he gets to his goal. The boy, sweating and panting and ready to give up, cries out that he has nothing left to give. But the coach barks, "Negotiate to find more strength!"

Finally, when the coach tells him he's made it and he can stop, the player collapses onto the ground, with the other boy still on his back. Panting hard and completely spent, the boy asks if he's made it to the fifty-yard line. The coach removes the blindfold and tells him the truth. He's crawled on his hands and feet across the entire 100 yards of the football field—twice the distance the coach originally asked him to crawl and more than he ever would have thought possible.

This scene is a perfect example of our limitless potential as human beings. Life has given us an incredible amount of talent. Unfortunately, most people never realize their true potential and hold themselves back by their own limiting beliefs. If you set your mind to something, give it your all, and never quit—and, most of all, believe in yourself—you will accomplish every goal and dream you have.

As the coach advises in the movie: "Don't quit… Don't walk around defeated… Don't waste your gifts." You have endless potential to fulfill every dream. Start becoming rich right now by accepting the fact that your potential is limitless.

BELIEF #6: Success requires change.

"It's never too late to change your life for the better. You don't have to take huge steps to change your life. Making even the smallest changes to your daily routine can make a big difference to your life."
— Troy T. Bennett

If you aren't willing to change who you are, what you believe, and how you do things, then your life will not change. Your financial situation, health, and happiness reflect how you have lived your life so far. Even though change may seem daunting, you must be willing to change what you believe and how you do things. Only then will your life improve.

Wealthy people embrace change and try to bring it about in their lives whenever possible because they know the secret: only by pushing yourself to try new things and taking risks do you create change, experience growth, and enjoy prosperity.

Change is your friend. Once you get comfortable with it and learn that becoming rich means changing many things about yourself, you will look forward to as much change as possible because it signals good things happening for you.

I have learned to love change because I've witnessed the abundance that comes with it. These days, I'm not happy unless something in my life is changing. I feel trapped and bogged down when things stay the same because I realize *change* is what brings me *growth*.

When you learn to think and act like a rich person, change will be positive and exciting. Start becoming rich right now by embracing and seeking change as often as possible.

BELIEF #7: Changing your life will not happen overnight.

"The only place you find success before work is in the dictionary."
— Vince Lombardi

You don't win, inherit, or steal success. Success is a lifestyle. Success is something you maintain. You don't buy success like you buy a car or a house. It is not a task and there is no finish line. It takes working smart and hard over time to change any aspect of your life. There is no such thing as a secret formula for success, happiness, or wealth.

Once you've arrived at your own version of success, then it's up to you to maintain it. The famous bodybuilder, actor, and politician, Arnold Schwarzenegger, said he built his life and success on "sets and reps." And the highly successful college basketball coach, John Calipari, famously expressed, "You have to learn to love the grind!"

Bill Gates and Warren Buffett, two of the richest people on the planet today, live the lifestyle of people who are continually building wealth. They will most likely continue to do this until the day they die. Why? It's what they do. They understand the philosophy of building wealth over time, accepting it, believing it, and buying into it. Wealth-building requires patience. There is no shortcut to success and happiness. It takes time and effort to change your life. And it's not a one-time job—it's a way of life.

Many people incorrectly believe that rich people are born with the Midas touch or they somehow got 'lucky.' All the rich people I know have earned their fortune by working smart and hard over time bringing value to other people. If you want to be able to think like a rich person, then you must remember that luck—or the lack of it—is not your problem. Instead, your belief systems have power—they have the power to lift you up and out of any situation.

Billionaire Warren Buffett started his wealth-building lifestyle at the age of nine, when he first began studying the stock market. He lived with the mindset of wealth for his entire life and finally made his first billion when he was 64 years old. Ray Kroc, the founder of McDonald's, didn't open his first McDonald's store until he was 56 years old. Similarly, Bill Gates quit college when he was in his early twenties to start Microsoft in his garage, and then didn't take a vacation for 20 years as he worked on developing his company. These billionaires did not get lucky; success was not handed to them. Instead, they earned every penny by working tirelessly over time, surrounding themselves with the right people, believing they could do it, and never quitting.

Another close friend of mine who built his success on his car dealership business, spent twenty long years working on his company. Again, he didn't just wake up one day to find someone had put a pot of gold at his door. Another friend and client took fifteen years to build up his 900-unit rental property portfolio. Even though he was able to quit his full-time job at the age of 35 he still works every day with a wealth-building mindset.

Creating wealth is a journey and a lifestyle, and it takes patience and perseverance to fully engage in this way of life. Please don't fall for the false promises of get-rich-quick programs, of which there are many. I have never met anyone who has used those plans and succeeded. The only person getting rich from those ideas are the people selling the idea. Trying to find that pot of gold at the end of the rainbow is a popular get-rich philosophy these days. These deceptive programs involve doing little or no work and putting in minimal time and/or require none of your own money. If these business concepts worked then why isn't everyone rich today?

Do you know how to move a mountain? One pebble at a time! There is no secret process or shortcut to success. It comes with small consistent changes every day that add up to massive changes over time.

I know many investors who work hard every day to acquire massive wealth over time. I have never met someone who drastically changed their standard of living with some secret formula—or without considerable time and effort. This is the most important message I can convey to you. You are not going to get rich overnight. It just doesn't happen. It takes time and effort to change your life. If you are serious about changing your financial place in life, then you should embrace this philosophy.

Start becoming rich right now by accepting the fact that working smart and hard over time, bringing value to other people, is the only way to acquire and maintain real success and wealth.

BELIEF #8: Now is the best time to start changing your life.

"Procrastination is one of the most common and deadliest of diseases and its toll on success and happiness is heavy."
— Wayne Gretzky

If you want to be rich, then stop wasting time. *Carpe diem*—seize the day! If you want to change your life, then there is no better time than the present moment to do it.

So many people suffer from 'analysis paralysis.' They make every excuse in the book to keep from taking chances or having to put in the extra work necessary to pursuing their dreams. The clock never stops ticking so you better get going right now. Stop waiting and making excuses. Procrastination is keeping you from living the life you deserve.

There will never be a better time to start changing your life. Next week or next year will not be better, or easier. Between now and then, life will present other hurdles. Don't wait until the kids are done with college or your divorce is final. Don't wait until you get some bill paid off or your tax refund arrives. All the opportunity, abundance, money, and technology are waiting for you— right now.

Now is the best time to start changing your life. Start becoming rich now and stop putting off pursuing the life you deserve.

BELIEF #9: Other people's actions and words have no effect on your decisions or your future.

"Your time is limited, so don't waste it living someone else's life. Don't be trapped by dogma, which is living with the results of another person's thinking. Don't let the noise of others' opinions drown out your own inner voice. And most important, have the courage to follow your heart and intuition."
— Steve Jobs

The day you stop worrying about what other people think or say about you and the choices you make is the day you can start increasing your happiness and abundance in all areas of your life. One of the most powerful shifts in thinking you can make is to start ignoring the naysayers and stop giving other people the power to make you feel bad.

The world is full of negative people who will make themselves feel good by making other people feel bad. It's likely you'll encounter these people as you make the necessary changes to become rich. These people will say you are turning into a snob and you're trying to be someone you are not. They'll say you're going to fail and lose everything. They will say you aren't smart enough. Whatever you do, don't lower yourself to their level. Don't criticize them back. They want you to fire back at them and become negative. Under all circumstances just let it roll off your back. These haters can only hurt you if you talk back to them or if they scare you into quitting. All this negative feedback from them is because they are scared and jealous.

Tell those who want to criticize that if they'd like to be in your life then they need to be supportive of your new goals. If these haters can't get onboard and cheer you on or even help you, then you might need to eliminate these negative people from your life. It will be hard at first, but it will be worth it.

The haters and doubters are going to show up. And, unfortunately, the people closest to us can sometimes be the biggest dream killers. They are jealous and feel bad because they don't know how to change their life. Our concern for what the people closest to us will say or think can cause more fear and paralysis than anything else.

I have been called delusional and grandiose because of the way I think. I love it now when people criticize me or doubt me. I've realized it is a sign of success. Think about it. The number one sports team in each of the professional sports leagues is typically either loved or hated. Their fans love them and the fans from all the other teams hate them. Not because they are bad people but because they are number one.

The haters will slowly disappear, and you will start attracting positive people who will empower even greater change in your life. Remember, what other people say or do has no control over your future.

You must stop giving other people the power and permission to make you feel bad. Another person can say whatever they want about you and it is meaningless unless you give it meaning. We all have the power to determine how we feel about what other people say about us or how they react to what we are doing.

If you let other people's opinions, statements, facial expressions, or body language bother you then you are giving away your power. If you are afraid of how other people will react to your goals or your dreams, you are just letting them steal your power. Don't be afraid of anyone. Keep your head down, stay in your lane, and take care of your business. As the great stoic Greek philosopher Epictetus said, "*If you want to improve, be content to be thought foolish and stupid.*"

BELIEF #10: Nobody owes you anything.

"A great burden was lifted from my shoulders the day
I realized that no one owes me anything."
— Harry Browne

No matter what has happened in your life, you need to accept the fact that nothing is owed to you. The world isn't at fault for where you are in life today and, by the same token, the world doesn't owe you anything. If you're waiting around for life to pay you back for something, it's going to be a long wait. The sooner you realize that your future is completely in your own hands, the better off you will be.

I don't care if your parents gave each of your siblings an inheritance, but they didn't give you anything. I don't care if all your neighbors won a million dollars in the lottery. I don't care if every one of your friends received full scholarships to Stanford and you didn't. Guess what? Life isn't fair. If you let it, life will keep kicking you until you decide to get out of the way of the kicking. If you are waiting around for something you think is owed to you, be prepared to keep getting kicked. Life will stuff you in a little box, close the lid, and put you on the shelf. The worst thing is nobody will care.

Stop holding out your hand for a freebie. It isn't coming. Your ship isn't coming in. The check isn't in the mail. The marines aren't on the way. People who are more successful or wealthy than you don't owe you their sympathy or a free lunch.

It amazes me how people will try to convince someone who has more money than them to give them money or buy them things. When I meet someone, who is more successful than me, my first thought is to buy them dinner or lunch so I can pick their brain. They are doing me the favor of sharing their knowledge, wisdom, and investment ideas with me. I'm the one who should pick up the check.

Another perspective that people have is that their employer owes them a pay raise just because they have been working the same job for the past ten years. This might come as a shock to you, but your employer does not owe you a raise. If you have been doing the same job for the past ten years without a pay raise, then you probably have not increased the value you are bringing to your employer. You are not worth more if you are doing the same thing you were doing ten years ago. Increase the value you bring to your employer and then they will give you a promotion and a pay raise. They don't owe you more if you don't do more.

It's time to stop waiting around and instead just roll up your sleeves and get to work. You can take complete responsibility for your future. Start becoming rich right now by accepting the fact that the world does not owe you a thing.

BELIEF #11: You either grow or you die.

"Step out of the history that is holding you back.
Step into the new story you are willing to create."
— Oprah Winfrey

On the surface this belief might sound a bit cruel. How can it be that your life is either getting better or getting worse, but not able to remain in its current state?

Most people seem to be happy the way their life is, and they don't believe they need to change it. They love their job, their family, their dog and the weekends playing golf and swimming in their pool. Their current annual income allows them to pay all the bills, contribute to their 401K, and take an annual vacation.

This sounds perfect. If it isn't broke don't fix it. Right? Unfortunately, today we live in a rapidly changing world. The rising cost of living, negative climate change, and the still unknown future impact of emerging technologies are going to create massive change across the globe. Economists predict the elimination of millions of jobs due to all this change.

The growth of Artificial Intelligence, robotics, automation, the global economy and the pending implementation of Block Chain technology alone will drastically change the employment landscape over the next few decades.

The increased cost of food, transportation, education, housing and health care have far outpaced the increase in workers compensation. If your income stays the same, then you are becoming poor just due to the rising cost of living. Financial analysts predict that 40% to 60% of people will not be able to afford to retire.

The gap between the richest few percent of people

and everyone else is staggering. Never in the history of the planet have so few people controlled so much wealth.

If you think your lifestyle is safe and insulated from this upcoming change, then it is time for you to become familiar with one of the most basic laws of the universe. The Law of Compensation. The Law of Compensation states that the amount of money or goods you receive in life is in direct proportion to these three things:

1. The demand for your skill set
2. How good you are at it
3. How difficult will it be to replace you

For example, the cashier at a fast food restaurant does not require any specialized education and her skill set is easily obtained. A fast food cashier can be trained in thirty days or less and almost any person can handle that skill set. In contrast to that, not many people can perform a heart transplant like a surgeon. A heart transplant surgeon goes to eight years of college and then interns under senior surgeons for years before they can do a transplant on their own.

I'm not saying everyone should go to school to be a doctor, but I am saying now is the time to assess what you do for a living. If your job can be replaced by a robot or kiosk, your income hasn't significantly changed in several years, and you have been performing your job with the same skill set for the past five years then it is time for you to realize you are dying, not staying the same.

The beliefs in this chapter are very powerful and liberating. If you accept them, they will break the chains of negativity and backwards thinking that are preventing your success. You will separate yourself from the masses when you believe, accept, and incorporate these beliefs in your life. Most people aren't even aware that their beliefs have the power to hold them back or propel them forward. I've seen in very real ways how a positive, wealthy mindset can take a person to the next level of accomplishment. The beliefs in this chapter are the foundation for prosperity and wealth in your life. Start becoming rich now by accepting and living by the beliefs in this chapter.

CHANGE IS GOOD

"If you want something you've never had,
you must be willing to do something you've never done."
— Thomas Jefferson

Every baby bird jumps out of the nest for the first time and flies. Even though they have never flown before and there is no guarantee that they'll be able to fly, they take that first tip-toe out of the nest and try it. They take the leap. If they don't, they won't become adult birds who can survive on their own—until they take that jump. Their lives won't start until they take that first scary risk of springing from the nest.

Once they make that leap—shall we say leap of faith? — they never come back to the nest. It can be very scary springing out of your comfort zone to make a substantial change in life. It's this fear of leaping that holds most people back from changing their lives for the better.

Understanding and implementing change is without a doubt the number one thing you must do if you want to become rich. The goal of this chapter is to drive home the point that change is critical, and you must embrace it. If you can make changes to your life, you'll be able to build wealth. No, it won't be easy. But if you want to change your education level, improve your health, increase your happiness, or become financially free, then you need to make significant changes in your thinking and actions and most likely implement a totally new way of living your life.

Transitioning to the thoughts and actions of a rich person requires massive change. I can only speak for myself when I say I had to change almost everything I was doing before I could start down the path to financial freedom. I improved my thoughts, words, and decisions. I completely modified the type of people with whom I was surrounding myself. I changed the entertainment content I was watching and listening to. I even adjusted the foods I put in my body, and when I went to bed.

So…you have a decision to make. If you want minor improvements to your life, then you will have to make some small changes. But if you want tremendous change in your life, then you must bring about huge changes in the way you think, act and live.

I have been willing to make extreme changes in my life and it's paying off as I watch my assets, cash flow, and net worth grow exponentially. I continue to purchase cash flow producing rental properties, and my real estate brokerage team continues to grow and prosper.

Change is a key word when it comes to talking about financial freedom and wealth-building. Unless you are currently as rich as you want to be, get ready to change the way you do almost everything in your life. You can wish for anything in life, but unless you change your beliefs, actions, thinking, and decision making, you won't change your outcomes. If you truly want success in your life, you must not only welcome change—you must demand it, fall in love with it, and make it your new lifestyle.

Drop the Approach Your Parents Used

My sister once said, "It's very hard to break out of the class you were born into." She was referring to the relationship between financial status and the belief systems you were raised with. If my siblings and I had continued to think like my parents, we would have done everything they encouraged us to do: pursue a college education (and then likely stop learning much of anything else after graduation), get a job, buy a house, and try to save money.

Unfortunately for most people, my sister's statement is too true. Unless most of us change the knowledge, belief systems, and work ethic we were raised with, our financial status won't be much different from that of our parents. Why? Because doing what most of our parents' generation did—finishing high school, working hourly jobs, and stuffing money under the mattress—is now an outdated belief system that doesn't work in our new world.

Even when you consider our 2.0 version of our parents' paradigm—college beyond high school, a salary instead of an hourly rate, and a 401(k)-retirement account to update the mattress approach—the method that worked in the past doesn't work any longer.

During the past 50-100 years our parents' encouragement to pursue a college education was the path to bettering yourself over their standard of living. For some of us, this post-high school education has led to a better life. But, regrettably, just getting a college education doesn't shift the fundamental way of thinking that needs to be thrown out. Along with the college degree, my generation and beyond also must deal with a higher level of consumer debt, households that require two incomes, higher levels of stress, and an exponential increase in divorce, foreclosure, and bankruptcies.

Most people fail to do financially better than their parents because they apply the same processes, beliefs, and knowledge that their parents used. The results are the same—or, in many cases, even worse. Using outdated belief systems may be the reason you're worse off than your parents were.

We now have a new world, with different rules. As such, many of us find that doing it the way our parents have always done it is no longer a sure track to success. If we don't change the mindset we learned from our folks, nothing will change for us, and my sister's statement--"It's very hard to break out of the class you were born into"— will be proved correct.

Fearing Change is Normal

Fear of failure is the main reason people avoid change and probably the biggest hurdle that stops people from reaching their goals. Entire books have been written about fear and overcoming it. In fearing that they will fail, many people will do nothing. Ironically, inaction means your future will most likely be unsuccessful since you're taking no active steps to make it better. So, in the end, you will have failed anyway.

Fear of failure is normal. I'm not saying if you experience fear you are weak or that you have a personality flaw. I experience fear all the time. Every successful person will experience fear throughout their life. It is unavoidable. One of the differences between people with an abundance/wealth mindset and those with a mindset of poverty is that rich people use fear to motivate them. Poor people let fear paralyze them. Fear is a good thing if you let it empower you.

If you talk to an elderly person about life, you will usually hear that their number one regret is that they were too afraid to act when an opportunity presented itself. Their regrets are always about something they *didn't* do.

In my own life, several instances came up when I had the opportunity to purchase a profitable rental property or even buy an existing business. However, I chose not to because of my fears: I didn't think I could afford it, or I didn't have the time to do it. Down the road I always wished I'd taken the chance and made those purchases when they were in front of me.

Steve Harvey, the popular talk show host, author, actor, and comedian, has become a very positive public speaker for self-improvement and transformation. He often says, "If you want to be successful you have to jump, there's no way around it. If you're safe, you'll never soar."

Fear is one of the biggest driving forces that keep me changing and growing. I don't want to wind up like my parents living paycheck to paycheck. My parents were awesome and gave me an incredible work ethic. But, sadly, they did not work smart and had no assets. They struggled to pay bills for their entire lives. I refuse to let my family and loved ones suffer because I can't afford to help them in times of need. I embrace my fear because it motivates me to change, grow, take risks, and get outside my comfort zone.

The Rich Love Change

People with money realize that change often brings opportunity. The most successful rich people don't wait for change—they create it on purpose. Rich people are poised for change so that they can capitalize on it when it happens. Rich people wait for stock market deviations so they can buy and sell stocks and mutual funds. Real estate investors made a killing during the 2006 through 2010 housing bubble burst by purchasing homes way below their market value, rehabilitating them, and then selling them for big profits.

The most successful and wealthiest people in the world make daily changes to their knowledge because they realize education is a big catalyst for success. Warren Buffett reads two to eight hours a day. Bill Gates goes away for a couple weeks every year just to catch up on his reading. Tai Lopez has become a multimillionaire by reading a book a day and then selling the most important knowledge he learns from each book to his coaching clients. When your level and value of knowledge increases, you will change your confidence level, beliefs, and actions. When that happens on a regular basis, your wealth will increase, and you will become rich. You can't grow your wealth without constant change.

Rich people are always trying to change their circle of influence. They want to meet as many people as possible because they know right around the corner is someone else who is going to present them with the next great idea or investment opportunity. If they widen their circle of friends, there's likely to be a mentor, a great coach, or a teacher who can help them learn a new or better way of doing things. Rich people associate networking with success.

Most people do not like change. Most people want the same job, the same house, and the same friends every day until they die. Change scares most people because they lack the confidence, experience, and knowledge to leverage change to their benefit.

Oftentimes people will spend most of their life with the same friends and family members. However, changing who you spend your time with is another key factor impacting your financial growth and success. If you don't grow your sphere of influence, you can't grow your wealth. Unless you are already hanging out with people who are smarter and wealthier than you, you need to start networking with people who want to grow their lives and wealth.

A famous statement that circulates in the business world really resonates with me: *You either grow or you die.* Rich people understand this concept and embrace it. They are always looking to change how they do things in order to improve on their habits. They are constantly working to add to their knowledge. And they work hard to consistently increase their assets and net worth. They do all of this because they know that standing still really means moving backwards.

People with a poverty mindset not only avoid change, but they fear it. One trait I have witnessed over and over is how people complain that life is not fair to them. They say they can't catch a break. I witness so many negative events and drama that can easily be avoided if people could take control of the changes and events in their lives.

One of my MBA professors said it best: *"Winners make it happen and losers let it happen!"* My hope is that this book will help you become a person who can make it happen and to create as much positive change in your life as possible. Change is scary because it means something different will happen—and some people might not have the confidence, experience, or knowledge to see that *different* could be *good.*

One of my favorite personal improvement gurus,

Jim Rohn, learned early in life that change was a necessary factor to success. When he was young, things weren't going very well for him. He was constantly strapped for money and things hadn't improved for him in five years. He discussed this with his mentor who asked him a series of questions. "How much money have you saved in the past year?" Jim answered, "Zero." The mentor then asked, "How many seminars have you attended in the past six months?" "None," said Jim. Next question: "How many books have you read in the past month?" Jim muttered, "none," again. The mentor paused and told Jim, "If I were you, I would stop doing that!"

Change is Inevitable

Change will certainly happen to you, no matter whether it is voluntary or involuntary. There are substantial changes on the world's horizon due to the ever-expanding global economy, climate change, advances in technology, and artificial intelligence. Many of the baby boomer generation can't afford to retire, and we have more consumer, credit card, and student loan debt than any time in the history of civilization. In the United States, bankruptcy and foreclosures are an accepted part of our financial landscape.

You have a choice to ride this wave of financial change and even benefit from it. If you resist or ignore this upcoming change, you will, in any case, change involuntarily. There is almost a certain chance that your quality of life, employment security, standard of living, and income will be impacted by these massive changes. You may even be swept aside by it because you chose not to prepare for the next level in life. Now is the time to prepare to benefit from this massive change.

We all face change whether we like it or not. If you decided to never voluntarily change a thing about your life, your circumstances will still change. Unfortunately, most involuntary change is negative change. There are several types of change, and you have the power to decide what kind of change will occur in your life.

When I was growing up there was a famous oil filter commercial by a company called FRAM. The commercial showed a car mechanic doing expensive repairs to a car because the owner had neglected to change their oil and oil filter at the right time. The famous slogan of the commercial was: "You can pay me now or you can pay me later." In other words, you can make the time now to get your oil changed, paying a small amount of money in the short term to avoid repair bills in the long term. Or you can pay a huge repair bill later when your car breaks down and you must fix it.

Life is like that commercial. You can take voluntary action now and benefit later or you can be subjected to involuntary action later—and pay the consequences.

Most change can be grouped into two categories: Voluntary change and Involuntary change. Every person will experience both types of change during their lives. Rich people are good at creating voluntary change and benefiting from it. Rich people are also good at being ready to deal with the challenges involuntary change can create.

Involuntary change

We all get older. We can't stop the years from marching on. Change due to aging is a form of involuntary change. It is involuntary because we have no way to stop or alter it.

Unfortunately, health problems crop up and create

extreme changes in people's lives. Chronic diseases like heart disease, cancer, arthritis, etc. can completely change the quality of a person's life and stop their ability to make a living. We have little control over these involuntary changes that can occur.

Accidents are another form of involuntary change. Nobody wants to be involved in a car wreck or a bad fall, but these types of unpredictable events happen to all of us. We cannot control other drivers making mistakes and crashing into us. Other times we get distracted when we are driving by texting, eating, smoking, or talking on the phone. Some people even drive while under the influence of alcohol.

Some of the ways rich people prepare and reduce the setbacks of involuntary change is by not taking the chances of being distracted when they are driving. If they get in an accident, they make sure they have current car insurance and their license and registration are up to date.

Something that is common with most rich people are their health habits. They have health and life insurance in place in case of an emergency and they pursue regular exercise and eat clean food.

It is predicted that over the next decade two million jobs performed by human beings are going to be eliminated due to the massive changes created by the robotics, artificial intelligence, and block chain technology. As companies downsize by leveraging these technology changes, people are going to lose their jobs. This is another form of involuntary change.

Sometimes uncontrollable events happen in our lives. When you learn to think like a rich person, you understand that you can't control everything that happens—but you can prepare and change how you react to it. Rich people can handle adversity and minimize the setbacks of involuntary change. They do not get financially or emotionally derailed by involuntary change.

Voluntary change

Voluntary change includes such examples as cutting back on the amount of sugar you eat, saving 10% of everything you earn, or choosing a book to read every month. It might mean making the change to pay your bills on time, brush your teeth, or maintain your vehicle on a better time frame.

Voluntary change is a desired experience if you want to be rich or at a minimum have a stress-free life. As I mentioned earlier in this chapter, deciding to avoid the situation and do nothing will not have a good result. When you avoid voluntary change, it will almost certainly result in involuntary change later. It is best to pay your bills, show up on time for work, and take care of your health. If you don't do these things you will eventually lose your income or wind up getting sick.

The difference between rich people and people with a poverty mindset is that rich people welcome and create voluntary change in their life. Rich people have a mindset that helps them deal with the involuntary change we all experience. Voluntary change is what makes you rich and adds money to your bank account and years to your life. Being able to deal with involuntary change is what allows you to avoid being derailed by life and quitting at the first sign of difficulty.

Rich people are always looking for ways to accomplish voluntary change when it comes to their income streams, emergency funds, and education levels. Rich people like to have more than one form of income in case one of their income streams goes away. They always have another source of income to fall back on. Rich people make continuous self-education a regular part of their life. They regularly read books, attend seminars, and pursue the advice of their mentor or coach. This voluntary change mindset of the rich is their hedge against financial involuntary change.

I am always growing my portfolio of rental property and increasing the size of my real estate agent team. I wrote this book to support a teaching, coaching, and speaking business. I will never stop this voluntary pursuit of change in my financial and business life.

Change is inevitable. You cannot avoid change no matter who you are. Neither the rich nor the poor can avoid change. Whether you are a billionaire, a president, or a king, you cannot avoid change. Even if you're one of the most beautiful people in the world or one of the most talented athletes, you still won't be able to avoid change.

The quality of your life and how certain world events impact you will all be based on whether you choose voluntary change now or become a victim of involuntary change later. By not choosing voluntary change you are choosing involuntary change. You can decide what kind of change you will see in your life.

Due to technology, massive change is on the way and it is up to you whether it is positive or negative for you. Your change can be voluntary or involuntary. If you stick your head in the sand and let life decide which type of change will happen to you, it will most likely be negative and involuntary: worse health, less job security, a smaller income, and more stress.

If you act now and make voluntary changes, you can increase your health, net worth, income, and happiness. You can do nothing and hope for the best and try to catch a break. The choice is yours. One thing I am 100% positive of is that you are going to change whether you like it or not. You can decide if the changes are positive or negative.

Make the decision to change now so your life can improve in every category. I am positive your life won't stay the way it is now. It is going to get better for you or worse for you, but it won't remain the same. Too much is happening now in the field of technology, education, medicine, and finance; all of us will be affected by these things in big ways. You can be a casualty of change or you can start planning your own future. You have complete control over which way it goes.

I know change is not easy. It is harder for some people than for others. I'm not going to sugarcoat it. Positive voluntary change takes time and commitment. Anything good in life, especially becoming rich, takes working smart and hard over time.

Change Requires You to Leave Things Behind

The explorer Hernán Cortés arrived in the New World in the year 1519 with 600 men and a fleet of ships. Upon arrival, he ordered that his men burn their boats. This sent a clear message to his sailors: *there is no turning back. You either win or you die.* Talk about motivation to succeed!

When I first decided to become a real estate sales agent, I was still working as a software developer so that I could keep the steady salary and good benefits. For 16 long months, I kept my full-time job while I was also working about 15 hours per week learning about selling real estate. When I finally decided to quit my position as a software developer, my sister thought I was nuts to leave a good, predictable job in order to take the risk of starting a new career in real estate. I only had a little money saved, but I had a few listings and a few deals under agreement. Although I wasn't sure how things would turn out, I believed in myself and knew I would do whatever it took to become a successful real estate agent. Because of my faith that things would work out fine, I ended up becoming a top-producing realtor for 16 years running and have founded my own brokerage company.

Despite the protests of my loved ones I took the leap, and I never went back to corporate America. In fact, I haven't had a 'real job' since that time. I burned my boat!

Sometimes you'll find that you must change jobs, improve your friends, quit unhealthy habits, leave a bad relationship, or give up things you like to do in order to have more time and positive energy to work on the life you want. Change might require you to experience some pain as you leave things behind. If you're unhappy with how your life is going, then maybe you need to burn your own boat and move on.

Below are ten easy, quick and free things you can change now to make an instant positive change in your life:

1. Drink more water and get at least seven hours of quality sleep every night.
2. Avoid eating processed sugar, diary, gluten, excess salt, and MSG.
3. Start getting some exercise on a regular basis.
4. Read at least thirty minutes a day.
5. Get out of debt.
6. Attend one seminar every six months.
7. Stop watching negative TV and Internet.
8. Avoid negative people who complain about everything.
9. Save 5% of everything you earn.

10. Join an investment club or your local landlord association or find a successful mentor.

LEARN FROM SETBACKS AND MISTAKES

"Failure is an event; it is not a person."
— Zig Ziglar

Failure only happens when you quit and give up. Only you can determine if you quit and fail at something. You have control over the outcome of your decisions and actions. Setbacks and mistakes are going to occur. These are normal events in everyone's lives. With the right planning and education, you can eliminate failure by greatly reducing the number of your mistakes and reducing the impact setbacks have on you.

Many authors, success mentors, and self-improvement speakers talk about failure and how it can be a great teacher. I prefer to focus on how to minimize the setbacks and mistakes that lead to failure. I believe failure is the outcome of quitting because you can't handle setbacks, or you make too many mistakes.

Another of my favorite quotes from Zig Ziglar is this: "You don't drown by falling in water. You only drown if you stay there." In other words, you don't fail because you make mistakes—you fail because you make the same mistakes over and over. Get out of the water, dry off, and don't repeat whatever caused you to fall in the water in the first place.

One of the biggest reasons most people fail to change their lives or fail to pursue their dreams is because they quit as soon as something goes wrong. Setbacks and mistakes are the number one reason most people fail and quit. In my opinion, it takes three to five years before most new businesses, investments, or career changes become successful. I guarantee that if you try to change your life to become rich, you will make mistakes and experience setbacks. The key is not giving up. If you don't give up, you will learn and grow from your mistakes and become rich.

Things happen. It is 100% certain you will experience problems no matter what you are pursuing in life. If you try to become rich, setbacks and mistakes will happen. It is not a matter of IF they will happen—it's a matter of WHEN.

Do you know what truly separates the winners from the losers, the owners from the employees, and the rich from the poor? People with a poverty mindset quit and accept failure way too early. They let problems shut them down. But rich people learn and grow from their inevitable setbacks and mistakes. They have backup plans, insurance, and diversification to handle the problems that arise.

What is a Setback?

A setback is an event that occurs in all our lives. Setbacks aren't something we cause intentionally or maybe even cause at all. Setbacks, whatever their source, are unpredictable. Below are examples of common setbacks we could potentially experience:

- You get a flat tire.
- You are involved in a car accident.
- You get stuck in traffic.
- A road you take to work is closed, and you're late for an appointment.
- Your home is robbed.
- Your identity, personal data or bank account is hacked or stolen.
- Your home is damaged from a storm or natural disaster.
- You get sick.
- You slip on the ice and break your leg.
- The economy goes bad and your business sales go down.
- You lose a loved one in an accident or to an illness.
- You are the target of a frivolous lawsuit.
- You drop your cell phone in water.
- The hard drive on your computer dies.
- You lock yourself out of your house.

Of course, you can make plans to avoid or minimize setbacks that may happen in your life. For instance, to avoid problems like your car breaking down, you can purchase emergency travel services like AAA. Then, even if you have a problem with your vehicle when you're on the road, you have a plan in place to easily fix the problem without having your entire world fall apart. You can also reduce headaches by having a good emergency car kit in your trunk and by learning how to fix a flat tire.

To cut down on stress from being late to things, you can make it a habit to leave early when you're heading out to an appointment or meeting. That way, even if you get lost, encounter heavy traffic, or have car issues, you'll still be on time. Don't exceed the speed limit or text and drive.

Don't load free software on your PC or open unfamiliar emails. Make sure you have good virus protection software on your PC, and you run a virus scan frequently. Save all your files to cloud storage such as OneDrive, Google Drive or Dropbox. This way if your hard drive on your computer goes bad you won't lose your files. Save all your passwords to a password protection phone app. Password protect your cell phone. Make sure your contacts are stored in MS Outlook or Google contacts. If you lose or destroy your cell phone, you won't lose your contacts. Check your bank accounts online daily.

Other things you can do to plan for all that life throws at you: purchase good homeowners and life insurance, always keep some cash in reserve for a rainy day, use legal corporations to shelter your personal assets from legal issues, make sure you hire and work with reputable people, install a security system for your home or business.

Even if you plan as much as humanly possible, though, setbacks will still happen to you. That's life. You do have a choice though if you want to minimize the number of occurrences. You also have a choice as to how quickly and easily you rebound from them.

Success suicide is a form of a setback that happens to people when they try to change their life and pursue big goals. It can be in the form of a physical injury, sudden accident, or even a self-destructive decision that happens to you right before all your hard work is about to pay off.

It usually happens when you are starting to see progress from all your efforts. Success suicide comes in many forms. It can be health problems, an accident, or a natural disaster. Success suicide is life's way of testing how serious you are about becoming successful. So many people let it derail their goals. The thing to never lose sight of is that success suicide is temporary. If you stay the course, don't quit, and work through it, life will reward you with your goals and dreams.

Michael Maher, author of *The Seven Levels of Communication,* put it this way; "It's the breakdown before the breakthrough."

Success suicide happened to me when I decided to become a better tennis player. When I was 25 years old, I gave up playing tennis. However, at the age of 50, I decided to get back on the court. I didn't want to just play the game again for fun. I wanted to play competitively in leagues and tournaments.

Over the past seven years, I have been committed to improving my tennis game. I purchased better rackets, I watch YouTube videos on how the pros play, and I train with a tennis pro once or twice a month. All this is working very well—my game has improved greatly. I play in tournaments and in a league. Best of all, as my game improved, so did the skill level of my opponents. When you start playing better tennis, better players are willing to play with you. That means longer points and having to run faster to get to balls that are hit with more speed. Unfortunately, this added more stress on my body—it didn't take long before I had a bad case of tennis elbow and the rotator cuff in my shoulder had become inflamed. After such success at tennis, I felt very frustrated at becoming injured.

At one point, I even had to take a month off from playing to let my body heal. When that happened, it would have been easy for me to just give up tennis and accept that I was too old to become a better player.

But I didn't give up. I stayed confident and kept believing that I could reach the level of play I dreamed about. I switched to an anti-inflammatory diet. I started playing fewer matches. All this helped me heal, avoid further injury, and get back on the court. The injuries passed, and my game continued to improve.

When you decide to change your life and become rich, setbacks will happen. You can't avoid this part of life, but you can have plans in place to handle the distractions, losses, and damage they cause. Always remember that the inconvenience, pain, or economic loss caused by these setbacks are temporary. Don't let them stop you from pursuing your dreams. *"Temporary setback"* must become an important phrase in your vocabulary if you want to become rich. Keep in mind that, though sometimes the sun is hidden behind the clouds, it is always shining. Eventually the clouds pass and the sun shines on you again. You have the power to decide how long you let a setback keep you from moving forward in life.

What is a Mistake?

A mistake is different from a setback because it is something we cause to happen through our actions, decisions, or beliefs. Most mistakes can be avoided when you think and act like a rich person. I'm not saying rich people don't make mistakes, but they do it less frequently than other people. And, when they do make mistakes, they know how to handle them. Another way a mistake is different from a setback is that mistakes can be predicted, minimized, or even completely avoided with proper planning, experience, and consulting with the right professionals. Also, having a great mentor to learn from will help you minimize the number of mistakes you make.

It is okay to make mistakes. In fact, it is quite normal and a crucial part of succeeding. All successful people make mistakes along the way. The one thing they all have in common is they did not quit. Studies show that most billionaires had a major financial meltdown before they became very successful and wealthy. It happened to me. I lost my entire net worth when I was 47 and had to completely rebuild my wealth. Because I learned so much from those mistakes, didn't repeat them, and didn't quit, I was able to rebuild my wealth ten times faster.

Your success in any endeavor in life is going to be determined by how well you learn from your mistakes, not how few mistakes you make. It's not a matter of if you will make mistakes—it's a matter of when. The main goal is to learn from other people's mistakes, so you don't make the same mistakes they made. Even with a great mentor, you are going to mess up. The key is to learn from your mistakes and avoid repeating them. Making a mistake once is okay. If you keep making the same mistake over and over, then you aren't learning from them. If you do that long enough, you will quit and fail. That isn't the outcome you want.

Every great entertainer, athlete, and entrepreneur makes mistakes. If you aren't striking out or getting hit by a pitch, then you aren't getting in the batter's box. You must be willing to strike out if you want the chance of hitting a home run. Every entertainer can tell you how they were booed off stage at some point in their career. Every entrepreneur has started a company that failed or made a product that didn't sell. One of the most common traits in successful entrepreneurs is that they've faced financial setbacks and made mistakes in their career before becoming rich. In the National Football League, half the tackles made during a game are made by a defensive player who was already knocked down on the play and got up off the ground to make the tackle.

Mistakes are good teachers because they have consequences. You suffer embarrassment, punishment, or some other penalty. When you are a kid and you do something wrong, your parents slap your hand. That's how we learn right from wrong. When you bounce a check, the bank slaps you with a fee. When you exceed the speed limit, you get a hefty speeding ticket. Some examples of mistakes we might make include:

- Texting while driving, drunk driving, or speeding.
- Cutting corners due to time constraints.
- Forming a business partnership with the wrong person.
- Marrying someone who isn't good for you.
- Not using a checklist to pack.
- Forgetting the grocery list.
- Using credit cards to solve financial problems.
- Not having car or home insurance.
- Neglecting to have an emergency fund or cash reserves.

My very first business venture was purchasing an Irish pub and restaurant with a couple of friends. We got into business together simply because we grew up with each other. However, it turned out our styles of management were completely different. After 10 years, we wound up going through an unpleasant business divorce.

When we formed our partnership, we'd neglected to create any kind of buy-sell agreement or dissolution clause. These terms and clauses would have spelled out how one of us could exit the partnership and how assets would be sold in the event of our relationship not working out. This chapter in my life was a huge mistake but an awesome learning experience. I can tell you with great certainty that I won't ever make those mistakes again. The next time I form a business partnership, I will get my attorney involved so he or she can make sure I do things right and I'm protected. I will also pursue business partners with similar short-term and long-term business goals.

When I purchased rental property for the first time, I bought it directly from the owner. Unfortunately, I didn't use a real estate agent and I had no professional inspections performed and I did not get an appraisal. After the closing, I found out the house had foundation, roof and plumbing problems and the seller had left it full of junk. It cost me $2,000 to remove all the junk and $15,000 to repair the foundation and plumbing issues. If I would have used a good real estate agent, they would have made sure I had the home inspected by a professional Home inspector and before closing we would have done a final walk-through to make sure that all the junk was removed by the current owner.

I haven't repeated those mistakes again. The important thing is I didn't quit investing in real estate just because of this costly set of mistakes. Instead, I used this experience to be a smarter investor going forward.

My business partners and I purchased a building for a night club project. We found out after the purchase that the building needed more repairs than we'd anticipated. Also, it had a ton of building code violations of which we were unaware. The building turned out to be an expensive lesson in real estate investing. When we purchased the building, we worked through the seller's real estate agent. That was a big mistake. We could have avoided this expensive real estate lesson if we'd had our own

ASSET #1: MINDSET

Commercial real estate agent representing us. Another thing we could have done would have been to ask an architect to walk through the building with us before we purchased it, so we were aware of building code issues. A great mentor or our own real estate agent would have advised us to find these professionals before we purchased the building.

I made many mistakes in all the above examples. I've neglected to find a great mentor to give me advice. I was nonchalant about hiring good quality professionals. I had no protections in place for when things went bad. And I stubbornly refused to pause my business dealings as I was learning so I continued to make the same mistakes over and over.

When I look back at all my mistakes and setbacks in life, almost all of them could have been avoided. That's why I'm so passionate about writing this book. I don't want this to happen to other people. The stories in these pages are my way of mentoring you so that you can learn from my mistakes on your own path to success. Inevitably, you'll make your own mistakes, too. That's okay. Making mistakes can be teaching moments on your path to success and can be priceless if you know how to learn and grow from them.

What to do When You Make a Mistake

What you do when you make a mistake will determine your success. Another trait of rich people is how they handle a mistake they've made. Not only do you need to learn from your mistakes, but you need to know what to do now that the mistake has been made.

When you make a mistake, don't make your situation

Page | 114

worse than it already is. When you make a mistake, don't be afraid to admit it. Mistakes can hang over your head and hold you back if you are afraid to admit to them. Accept responsibility as soon as possible and work it out with whoever the mistake is affecting. If you lie about it or blame someone else, then you are making more mistakes. When you're in a hole, stop digging.

I've faced many times when I've made a mistake and then was afraid to tell the person it was affecting. I was afraid they would be hurt or angry—or maybe not trust me anymore. Sometimes, I was afraid of being embarrassed. During these times, I would try to come up with some excuse or story to get me out of having to tell the truth and look bad. However, every time I tried to fake my way out of it, I regretted not telling the truth. The day I grew up and started acting like a rich person, I made a commitment to myself to tell the truth as soon as possible and work as hard as I could to make the situation right. I soon realized that facing my mistakes and trying to solve the problem as quickly and ethically as possible is so much easier of a path. It was better to tell the truth and look bad... than it was to lie so I could look good.

When you make a mistake, don't compound the problem by doing the wrong things. Don't lie about it or try to hide it. Blaming other people and refusing to take responsibility for the mistake is not the solution either. Do not delay your efforts to resolve the mistake. Most importantly, don't quit or give up on your goal or plan.

My best advice is to immediately accept responsibility for the mistake and own up to it with the person or people it is affecting. Be completely honest about how the mistake happened. Do everything in your power to correct the damage or make up for the mistake.

Do not quit or give up on your goals and plans just

because you make a few mistakes. Think about the chain of events or decisions you made that led to the mistake. Think about what you will do in the future, so you don't repeat that mistake again.

The bottom line is this: we all make mistakes. Make sure you learn from them. Don't repeat them. Accept responsibility as soon as possible and be willing to clean up your mess.

Why Do We Quit Too Soon?

I believe there are several reasons people quit pursuing their goals and dreams too soon. First, they just don't know any better. Second, it is easy to quit. Third, they don't have a good mentor to help them through the tough times.

The first reason people quit too soon on their goals and dreams is because they don't know any better. They don't realize that if they don't quit, they will succeed. In fact, many of them are close to succeeding when they give up. Earl Nightingale is a legend in the self-improvement industry. He has a cartoon drawing in one of his teachings that shows a man in a diamond mine digging for diamonds with a pick. The man can't see it, but the diamonds are just a few swings of his pick away. The man is frustrated and tired. He is about to give up looking for the diamonds. He doesn't know any better, but he would find the diamonds if he just tried a little longer.

The second reason people quit too soon is because it is easier to quit. Quitting is an instant form of gratification and gives you an instant sense of relief. When you quit, it removes the pressure and stress of trying to change your life and step outside your comfort zone. You can go back to your ordinary life and rid yourself of the worry and challenge that goes along with trying to be rich and successful. Unfortunately, this quitter's gratification is very short-term. Eric Thomas is an international success and motivation guru who said, "You're already in pain. You can quit now but you will be in pain for the rest of your life. If you don't quit, you can get a reward for your pain."

That is a very accurate view of quitting. If you quit too soon, you'll regret it forever. But if you don't quit, you will succeed and enjoy the rewards forever.

Third, people quit because they don't have a mentor. I can promise that a great mentor won't let you quit! That person will help you handle the tough times, resolve setbacks, and learn from mistakes. They'll discourage you from taking the easy way out. They will motivate you, hold you accountable, and help you stay calm when the going gets rough. When you have a mentor, he or she can help you see the big picture so that you can learn from your mistakes. This mentor can also help you adjust your path so you can continue pursuing your goals.

If you asked me the number one trait that has made me successful, I would say it's my ability to persevere. This is the single biggest reason I have become successful. I don't let setbacks and mistakes stop me anymore. I experience problems just like everyone else, but I don't quit. I am no smarter than anyone else and, yes, I make plenty of mistakes. However, I never think about quitting. I accept each mistake as a lesson on my way to becoming rich. This is one of the big differences between those who think with an abundant mindset and those who don't. Rich people don't panic and quit when something doesn't go their way.

Before I learned to think like a rich person, I specialized in failing and quitting. Below is a list of experiences and opportunities I quit on too soon:

- I have sold off income-producing real estate to remove stress from my life instead of removing the real source of the stress.
- I switched or quit jobs for the wrong reasons.
- I started my first seminar business then shut it down after one year because it didn't make enough money.
- I quit college after my first year because I was lazy and partying too much.
- I shut down a Realtor coaching business before it even got off the ground.
- I started a real estate licensure business and then shut it down after one year.

At the time I was making these decisions, I had a loser mindset. I wanted instant results. I would get frustrated when the first setback or mistake came along. I would let other people convince me something was a bad idea. I didn't realize you have to work hard and smart over time bringing value to other people. I did not know that it takes three to five years before a new business or idea becomes successful. I did not leverage other people's time, knowledge, and money. I had no mentor to talk to when things weren't going my way.

I would get scared that I was wasting time and money on an idea or business that might not succeed. I didn't realize it takes time for any venture to become profitable and run with momentum. The reason I quit is because I didn't know any better. I did what most people would do when things go wrong. I took the easy way out and ran away from the opportunity. Every time I quit, I felt that instant relief from the pressure of trying to start a business or pursue an opportunity but always regretted later that I had quit too soon.

Eighty percent of all businesses fail within the first five years. Think about that. This corresponds with my belief that it takes three to five years for a new business to become successful. I wonder how many of those failed businesses would have succeeded if the owner had just hung in there a little longer.

Don't Let Past Mistakes Be Future Problems

What do you do about mistakes you have made in the past that are still hanging over your head? Some of these bad decisions can haunt you and hold you back. If you truly want to change your life and become rich, it's important to address these issues, so they don't get in your way later. If you want to move forward in life and become rich, you don't need past mistakes weighing you down.

We've all made mistakes and experienced failure in our past. And most of us have been hurt or disappointed by someone else, too. But harboring negative feelings of animosity or sorrow will not serve you. If you've mistreated people, it's up to you to try to resolve those issues. If someone is harboring negative feelings and animosity toward you, that, too, will get in your way sooner or later. Dwelling on the negative past can cause stress, anxiety, and insomnia. These are not the traits of a successful entrepreneur or a rich person.

Make the decision to forgive yourself and others for anything that went wrong in your past. If you want to become rich, you must move on and start a new life. This requires thinking positively and surrounding yourself with positive people. Don't let your past control your future. In the book, *The Power of Intention,* Dr. Wayne W. Dyer talks about letting go of your past and using the power of intention to break free of the negative effects that people can have on us.

Many of us have skeletons in our closet. This could be a mistake or some bit of bad judgment that you made in your past that you regret for some reason. Skeletons can come back and make your life difficult, so I'd recommend cleaning out your closet. You don't want to work hard to change your life and become rich only to have something from your past come up and stop you.

You might have a skeleton in your closet if there is someone you don't want to see at the grocery store or movie theater because of something you did or said to that person, if there's someone you don't want to run into when you are on a first date, or if there's someone you don't want to sit next to at a holiday dinner. Skeletons in your closet are distracting and have an amazing way of biting you in the butt at the worst possible times. When these past mistakes are lurking in the back of your mind, they take your focus off doing what it takes to succeed. They bring you back to a place where you don't want to be. They must be cleaned up, so they cannot run free to steal your confidence and concentration. Cleaning the skeletons from your closet allows you to totally focus on doing what you need to do so you can get where you want to go.

For example, if you borrowed money from someone and never paid them back, you must always worry about running into that person. When you start to become successful, the person you owe money to will probably say terrible things about you. This bad reputation could stop you from landing an excellent job or convincing an awesome mentor to work with you. Instead of facing these embarrassing scenarios, have the courage to call the person who loaned you the money and apologize for not paying them back. Agree to repay them back even if it is a small monthly or weekly payment. You'll be amazed how a little effort on your part can salvage broken relationships and let you walk once again with your head held high.

How to Repair a Lost Relationship

Identify the people with whom you have the most unresolved issues. These could be past relationships, employers, business partners, friends, family, or coworkers. These are people you avoid talking with and running into. They could be people who have hurt your feelings or people you let down in the past.

Contact each person. Invite each of them separately to a coffee shop or some other non-threatening, alcohol-free environment. Tell each person that you want to apologize for allowing things to get bad between the two of you. Even if you feel they are at fault, tell them you want to move on. Some may doubt your intentions but tell them that you sincerely feel it is time to clear the air. Ask those who agree to meet to write down any ways they think you wronged them, and you do the same. Tell them to bring this list to your get-together.

Show up on time and thank the person for being gracious enough to meet with you. Tell that person that you want to apologize for whatever you did that hurt them (even if you don't completely agree with their view of the situation). Be an adult. Finger pointing only tears people apart.

Keep in mind that the way you remember how things happened in the past might be totally different from their memory. Listen to each issue they have with you. Don't interrupt them when they are talking. Try to see it from their perspective. Seek to understand why they harbor bad feelings toward you. Apologize for each thing they think you did to wrong them. If you're nervous about apologizing, go ahead and practice in a mirror before each meeting.

At the end of the conversation, thank them again for talking with you. It was a big show of faith on your part to try to patch things up. Plus, they are helping you to move toward your dreams by tying up loose ends from your past. The next day, send them a handwritten card thanking them for their time. You can then decide if you want to stay in touch going forward. After you tie up your first loose end, you'll want to resolve them all. This is hard to explain until you have done it, but once you do, you'll know what I mean. I learned so much about myself by tying up my loose ends. This process has helped me become a more understanding and patient friend.

Everyone makes mistakes and experiences setbacks. Setbacks happen to all of us. Be prepared when these setbacks occur so you can minimize the amount of time and money you lose when it happens. It is normal and okay to make mistakes. These are not failures. They are learning experiences on the way to success. Make sure you learn from your setbacks and mistakes and don't repeat them. Don't let these things force you to quit too soon. Let your mentor help you through the tough times and maybe even teach you how to avoid mistakes and deal with setbacks. Lean on your mentor to motivate you to not give up and to continue to pursue your dreams and goals. If you decide to change your life and become rich, take the time to go back and clean up past mistakes. Don't let something from your past derail your dreams and goals.

HAVE WRITTEN GOALS AND PLANS

"If you want to be happy, set a goal that commands your thoughts, liberates your energy, and inspires your hopes."
—Andrew Carnegie

A goal is something you wish to obtain or accomplish sometime in the future. It includes an effort that one makes toward some result or achievement. A goal can involve changing some aspect of your life or maybe removing something from your life. Your goal could be to acquire something you don't currently have or in some way improve your health, wealth, or happiness.

Goals can be educational, financial, social, or income-related. Goals can be long-term, where you set a deadline for yourself to accomplish something. Your goal might be retirement-related. Or a goal can be as short-term as wanting to get your grass cut tomorrow or get a raise at work before the end of the year.

A goal is a clear idea of what you want to accomplish. They represent where you want to go. Even if you don't know how you are going to get there, it is critical that you clearly define where you want to go.

First, you must know what your goals are. Goals are central to achieving success in any endeavor: business, sports, education, relationships, etc. I truly believe that writing down our goals is something we should all do. I almost *always* obtain the goals I write down whereas I usually *don't* obtain the goals I don't write down.

Goal setting is central and critical to success in changing your life and becoming rich. Without goals, you cannot go from being poor to becoming rich. It's simply not possible to become rich without goals. The desire to become rich can be the highest-level goal for many of us.

Goals can have a time period attached to them or be an ongoing desire to increase or decrease something. They can focus on accomplishing something positive or discontinuing something negative in your life. Examples of goals for some of us might be:

- Removing a negative toxic person from your life.
- Bench pressing 200 pounds.
- Losing ten pounds.
- Reading one book a month.
- Getting your GED or going back to college.
- Lowering your blood pressure.
- Developing enough passive income to quit your job.
- Earning $10,000 a month before you are 40.
- Retiring by the age of 50.
- Starting your own business.

Goal setting is critical for any person, team, or company to succeed and grow. When you decide to change something in your life, you are setting a goal. Changing what you do with your time, what decisions you make, how you spend money, and who you surround yourself with are all part of the goal setting process. When you do these things, you're usually trying to accomplish something big. To accomplish big goals, you must be good at setting and accomplishing a lot of smaller goals. Without the ability to set and obtain a series of small goals, you will not change anything big in life.

My Ten Steps to Accomplishing Any Goal

What follows is a list of points to consider when you're trying to achieve your goals. These are based on my own life experiences, the books I have read, and the seminars I've attended. My hope is that these ten steps will greatly increase your chances of acquiring the goals in your own life.

STEP 1: Make your goal realistic.

Crazy goals are probably not going to happen. For instance, if you say you want to be a billionaire in three months, you're most likely setting yourself up for failure. However, a goal to save $60,000 in five years is clearly defined and reasonable. It's specific and has a realistic time frame attached to it. Try to resist setting goals that are so challenging that you'll never be able to accomplish them. As we discussed earlier, you eat an elephant one bite at a time. Use this same approach to accomplish a big goal.

When I became a real estate agent, my career goal was to sell 50 houses in one year. I decided to accomplish this goal within a five-year timeframe. I broke down this sales goal as follows:

Year One — sell 15 houses
Year Two — sell 25 houses
Year Three — sell 35 houses
Year Four — sell 45 houses
Year Five — sell 50+ houses

To help me accomplish the increased sales each year, I wrote down and updated my own 'goal sheet' every November. This way, I would have a new set of written goals for the upcoming year. Later in this chapter, I will talk about what the main goals are on my goal sheet. These incremental and realistic goals allowed me to have continued steady success. At the end of my fifth year as a full-time real estate sales agent, I reached my goal when I sold 54 houses!

Another goal of mine was to earn $100,000 a year in gross income. I reached that goal in my fourth year as a full-time real estate sales agent. Now my next goal is to earn $100,000 a month from all my revenue streams. When I accomplish that, my next goal will be to earn $250,000 a month in revenue. I'm describing my own goals to illustrate the fact that you must learn to walk before you can try to run.

If you are making $10/hour at your job and you decide to earn $250,000 a month, you are setting your sights very high. I don't want to be a dream killer but that is a big jump in income. I want you to be successful. A better goal would be to double your income and get to $20/hour. Once you are earning that, then you can set the next goal: $50/hour! I find this incremental goal setting approach is highly successful for most people. Slow and steady surely wins the race.

In 1970, NASA decided to put a man on the moon. NASA set that goal first before they decided to design and launch the space shuttle or the Mars rover. Big goals are always a series of smaller goals accomplished one at a time and in the proper sequence.

STEP 2: Make sure your goal is specific and well-defined.

It's important that you know specifically what you want to accomplish so, from the start, you can head in the right direction. If you know you want to drive to New York City to see the Statue of Liberty, you have clearly defined a goal. You might not know every road to take to get there, but you know your end point. You can't just aim in the general direction of the East Coast—that's not clearly defining your goal. Nor can you say you just want to go to New York City—that's not definitive enough, either. Where exactly is it you want to go? If you recognize that you want to specifically go to the Statue of Liberty, you can plug the exact address into Google Maps, and it will tell you every street, road, and turn to take.

Changing your life and becoming rich is like driving to the Statue of Liberty. The most crucial step is having a precise goal that you are passionate about. Without this first step being clear-cut, you can't succeed with the remaining steps. If you don't know where you are heading, then how can you get there?

This step requires you to know exactly what you want. The more specific your goal is, the better chance you have of accomplishing it. Saying you want to be a millionaire is not explicit enough. An example of a better way is to say it like this: "I want to own 50 rental units within five years that produce $10,000/month in cash flow."

If you want to start a YouTube channel, you wouldn't just tell yourself you want to have the best sports channel. Instead, you'd more specifically shoot for having 50,000 subscribers by the end of the second quarter of 2021. Other examples of clearly defined, realistic goals would be to bench press 200 pounds by the end of the year or to lower your cholesterol total to less than 200 milligrams/deciliter within 12 months. Or it might be to save 10% of every paycheck you earn by the end of this year or to get yourself out of debt within two years.

Specific. Clear. And reachable.

STEP 3: Set a specific time period or date to accomplish the goal.

As you can see in the examples above, I added a deadline to each. This is important. Without a timeframe for your goal, you can't create much of a plan. If you don't set definitive deadlines, then you will most likely kick the can down the road, procrastinating and pushing off the beginning of your new life.

The best example of this is when I was trying to obtain my real estate brokers license. I had completed the coursework and the sales qualifications. All I had to do was take the state and national exams. I had a very thick textbook, lots of paperwork, and tons of notes to study. I decided to study for a few weeks then set the date to take the exam.

Well, days turned into weeks and weeks turned into months because I had no clearly defined date or timeline set for when I would take the exam. Every day I procrastinated about studying because I felt too busy. Who cared if I didn't take the exam? I didn't have any sort of penalty putting fire under my feet. I wasn't worried about it.

Eventually I realized I wasn't accomplishing my goal of passing the exam. That's when I knew I had to get focused and set a date to take it. So, I created a study plan in writing, making a list of the 40 chapters I needed to learn. I wrote the date on the plan for when I would study each chapter. I decided to study one chapter per day. That meant it would take me 40 days to cover all the material. I added five extra days for study time in case I missed a day or needed a break.

With this schedule in hand, I went online and scheduled the test. In 45 days, I'd be taking the exam, whether I was ready or not. When I scheduled the exam online, I had to pay for it and there were no refunds—the pressure was on! I had *"burned my boat"* and now I had to perform. With my 45-small, easy-to-accomplish daily goals, I studied my heart out because I now had the motivation I needed. Forty-five days later, I passed the test.

Whenever I participate in seminars or courses, I always attend them live in a classroom with an instructor. This way I have a specific day and time to be in attendance. Live courses have set dates and times when you must be there. If you don't show up, then you don't take the course. I don't do well with online learning because it is too easy to keep putting off sitting down and doing the work. As a side bonus, I prefer live classrooms because I get to network with the other attendees and the instructor.

Set a written deadline for your goal so that you can monitor your progress and plan your timeline. Also, if you have a mentor or a sponsor, they can help you measure your progress and hold you accountable for it. This is huge when you are trying to accomplish big goals.

STEP 4: Put your goals in writing.

Studies have proven that writing down your goals can increase your chances of achieving them by 40-50%. Also, when you write down your goals, you activate parts of your brain that would not otherwise be involved when you just *think* about doing something. Writing is an additional form of learning that helps commit information to our subconscious mind even further.

As you write down your goals, they become more

recognizable, more spelled out, and more realistic to you. The morning ritual of writing in a journal exactly what you want in life and saying it out loud is extremely powerful. You can rewrite your goals every single day as part of your morning ritual. When you write them down, you continue to reaffirm in your subconscious mind that you strongly desire your goals and that you are serious about obtaining them. This is very powerful.

STEP 5: Break your larger goal into a set of smaller goals.

Goals form the strategic plan that tells you where you want to go and how you will get there. A plan is a set of written steps or smaller goals you will execute to accomplish the greater goal. Now that you know where you want to go, your plan will determine how to get there.

The story I told earlier about how I accomplished passing my real estate broker exam is a good example of how you break down a big task into smaller pieces with dates and times. I broke down that goal into daily tasks that made it easy to accomplish. Any huge objective can be completed by breaking it down into smaller steps with a written schedule for being finished. It helps tremendously if you break down your goal into measurable steps and have a system to track your progress.

Let's say your goal is to save $60,000 over the next five years. Initially that might sound like a huge task, but it looks a lot easier if you break it down. The first step is to break it down into smaller amounts, with specific time periods or dates. This would be the same as $12,000/year or $1,000/month. So now the big goal becomes a series of 60 small goals of saving $1,000 a month.

Add up all your bills and the things you need to

spend money on and then subtract that amount from your monthly paychecks. If you don't have $1,000 left over, then you need to decide what spending you will cut so you have $1,000 surplus at the end of each month.

STEP 6: Read your goals out loud to yourself every day.

Now that your goal is clearly defined, written, and broken down into smaller steps with dates, it is time to use your written goals and act. Your objectives must be constantly at the top of your mind. It's great to keep your written set of goals visible to you so that you can read them out loud to yourself at least several times a day. If you can do this, you'll start to generate positive thoughts, motivation, and action. Your goals must always be on your mind. You want to see them at the start of your day and at the end. If you repeatedly read your goals, you can't help but act toward making them a reality. Your subconscious mind will take over and make things happen.

Any system of writing them down really will work. Here are some ideas for where to write your goals so that you can read them every single day:

- Sticky notes stuck to your bathroom mirror or your car dashboard.
- Index cards on your nightstand.
- A screen saver on your computer.
- The screen saver photo on your cell phone.
- Wet erase board on your office or kitchen wall.
- A small card you keep in your pocket.
- On your hand with permanent marker if that helps!

Of course, one of the best places to write and read your goals is in the Money Playbook. Use one of the Goal sections to write down all the details of your goal. Cut and paste photos into the Money Playbook or your Vision Board if it helps. Read the details of your goal and view the photos every day. Think about the changes that will occur in your life. Imagining the feeling of how your life will be after you accomplish your goal is very powerful. These positive conscious and subconscious thoughts that come from this exercise can lead a person to take massive action to achieve their goal.

Manifesting your goals is all about reminding yourself over and over what you want in life. You need to see your goals, say your goals, and think about your goals as often as humanly possible. You want to cement your intentions deep into your conscious and subconscious mind. The famous personal improvement guru Earl Nightingale said it best: "*Whatever we plant in our subconscious mind and nourish with repetition and emotion will one day become a reality!*"

STEP 7: Decide what you will sacrifice to accomplish your goal.

Most goals will require you to make some sacrifices. Let's take the goal above of saving $60,000. What expenses and luxuries are you willing to cut out of your regular spending to free up money, so that you have $1,000 to put in savings at the end of each month? Some ideas for saving money here and there to accomplish this particular savings goal might be: stop frequenting expensive cafés, pack a lunch to take to work instead of eating out, cancel your cable, cook more and eat out less, lose expensive habits like gambling and drinking alcohol, share a car with someone else in your household, withhold some spending on furnishings or clothing for a year, and opt for a 'staycation' instead of an expensive vacation.

Most things in life that are worth having require some hard work and sacrifice. This list of the price you are willing to pay should also be written down. Use the Goals section of the Money Playbook to write down these sacrifices. In this way, you'll be able to see it every day and start to understand how these sacrifices can get you to your goals.

STEP 8: Determine when you will work on your goal.

Not only do you need a timeline or date for when you want to accomplish your goal, you also need a written schedule for when you will work on your goal. If you don't have a written agenda blocking out specific time to work toward your target, life will repeatedly get in the way.

When I was studying for my broker's exam, I set aside one-hour right after lunch to study. I studied from 1-2 p.m. every day. I blocked this time out in my Google calendar, so it was spoken for in my day, and looked at it as being just as important as any other appointment.

Say, for instance, you want to watch an online course about multi-level marketing. If this is something you'd like to do, then you need to block out the time for it. Write it down on your whiteboard in your kitchen, in your personal schedule, or on your Google calendar—set an appointment with yourself for the exact day and time you'll watch it. Be specific, write it down, and make it your priority. Be as unambiguous as possible as to what you will do and when you will do it. If a friend calls and wants to get together, tell them you already have plans. If something is important to you, then you need to stick to your schedule to make sure that it happens.

It is important to be productive as possible when you are trying to accomplish big goals. Make sure you won't be distracted when you are working on your goals. If you can't work from home because the kids and pets want your attention, then find a location where you won't have interruptions. A local Coffee shop is a great place to stay focused. You can stay at work one hour longer if that helps. If you are starting a new business, consider paying for access to shared office space. Many cities now have shared office concepts. You pay a minimal fee and get access to all the services you need to start a new business. Just Google Shared Office Space to find these locations.

STEP 9: Create a system to track your progress.

To achieve any goal, you must have a system for writing down and tracking your progress. This will help you to understand how you're doing. You need to know your progress and if you are meeting the timelines for each step towards the goal. The best example I can give you is the use of scoreboards at sporting events. The scoreboard tells the players whether they are winning or losing… if they're ahead or behind. Your goal scoreboard will tell you the same thing. You need to track your progress, or you won't be able to tell if you're on target to accomplish your goal.

At sporting events, entire game plans are constructed and altered because the players know what the score is. If a football team is behind in the score and there are only a few minutes left in the game, they start throwing long passes and taking bigger chances with their offensive play calling because they now need to score more points in less time.

Again, let me use the story of when I was studying to take my broker exam. I had a written list of each module I had to study and the date and time I would study it. Each day I studied I drew a line through the completed module on my written list. Each day, I could clearly see what I'd accomplished. The list was my game plan and my scoreboard. If I studied the module that day, then I would cross it off my list. I could tell just by looking at my list whether I was on schedule or not.

Some good systems of creating a goal scoreboard are writing down each step of your goal in a notebook, writing the steps and dates on a whiteboard in your kitchen or office, or taping a printed MS Excel spreadsheet to your bathroom mirror.

Personally, I think using a whiteboard in a kitchen or office is the best goal scoreboard. It is big, easy to read, and hard to miss. You also tend to walk past it several times a day. It will allow other people to see it and cheer you on while you are trying to reach your goal. The person who is holding you accountable will also be able to monitor your progress.

Below are a few examples of a whiteboard scoreboard. You put an X in each square if you accomplish that task for the day. At the end of the week, you total up each row and then add the row totals to get the grand total score. Since there are seven tasks you are trying to accomplish over seven days, a perfect score would be 7 x 7 = 49. In your first week, you probably won't score 49 but the scoreboard tells you how far off you are, what areas you must work on, and if you are improving.

Healthy Eating / Diet Scoreboard

TASK	Mon	Tues	Wed	Thur	Fri	Sat	Sun	TOTAL
Read & write morning rituals	X			X		X	X	4
Eat a healthy breakfast	X		X	X	X	X	X	6
Work out	X		X			X	X	4
Drink 4 glasses of water		X		X	X	X		4
Do 1 hour of cardio				X		X	X	3
Only eat 1500 calories				X	X	X	X	4
Eat less than 20 grams of sugar					X	X		3
							GRAND TOTAL	28

Exam Studying Scoreboard

TASK	Mon	Tues	Wed	Thur	Fri	Sat	Sun	TOTAL
Get out of bed at 6:00 am								
Read & write morning rituals								
Eat a healthy breakfast								
Study for 1 hour before work								
Study for 1 hour at lunch time								
No TV/social media after work								
Study 1 hour before bedtime								
							GRAND TOTAL	

You must make your goals your priority. There is a great saying in the real estate sales business: *Don't plan your prospecting around your schedule—plan your schedule around your prospecting.* The point is that you should perform the most important tasks in your life first and then do everything else after that. So, in the same way, we could say this: *Don't work on your goals around the rest of your life activities—plan your life activities around your goals.*

If your goal is to read the paper every morning to find real estate deals, then do that every morning before you do anything else. Before you take your shower or have your breakfast, you must read the paper. Start the rest of your day only after you have scoured the paper for deals, new jobs, etc.

So much time can be wasted if you constantly switch your priorities and bounce from task to task, project to project, and goal to goal. An example of this, again, is when I kept procrastinating about taking my broker's exam. One day I was having lunch with my good friend, Lesia, who is a very successful executive coach. When I told Lesia I was trying to get serious about this test, she told me very definitively, "Don't put time into anything else or work on another project until you pass that test. Don't plan more meetings, don't work on your book, don't analyze and purchase another rental property, and don't give another person any of your time until you pass your test."

She was right. I was letting myself be pulled in ten different directions. I never felt like I had the time to sit down and study. I wasn't making this test my most important priority. From that moment forward, I did not make another meeting or appointment or do much of anything else until I took the exam.

The funny thing is, Lesia called me a couple of weeks after she gave me the advice and asked me to help her with a fund-raiser her Rotary club was doing. I told her I wasn't allowed to put another event on my schedule or be able to help her until I passed my exam. She laughed and called me a colorful name, in fun of course.

As I mentioned earlier in this chapter, I broke down my goal into realistic smaller goals and dates. I generated a written plan with dates and times and set a completion date by which to accomplish my goal. I paid for and scheduled my test in advance, so I had a date by which to accomplish the big goal. I crossed off each smaller goal on my written list, as I completed them. This list of crossed off smaller goals acted as my scoreboard to tell me how I was doing. I made the big goal my number one priority by blocking out all other time distractions. Thanks to Lesia's advice and using the steps outlined in this chapter, I was able to study for and pass my exam in exactly 45 days.

Everything that can be realistically put off must be put off if you truly want to make your goal a priority. To be clear here, I don't mean put off eating or sleeping or interacting with your family, but anything that can wait must wait if you want to make your dreams come true.

STEP 10: Find someone to hold you accountable.

It's extremely helpful to have a person in your life who is willing and capable of holding you accountable in completing your goals. Accountability is a powerful tool to help a person change their life. If you hire a coach in the executive, sales, or fitness area of your life, this coach is going to hold you accountable for your actions and monitor your progress. If this coach gives you tasks or goals to complete and you don't do them, they are going to want to hear why you didn't do what you said you were going to do. Finding or hiring someone to be your goal setting coach can be a huge asset when it comes to finding success.

Remember when you were in grade school or high school and the teacher gave you a homework assignment? You knew the teacher was going to call on you the next day to share your answers. If you didn't do the homework, you would have been embarrassed in front of the class. This potential embarrassment and accountability to the teacher was motivation to do your homework.

Finding a trusted person to hold you accountable is a critical and valuable step in accomplishing your goals.

The Ten Big Goals Every Person Should Set

As you can tell, goal setting is a substantial part of my life and it has allowed me to find much success. Below is a list of goal categories I use to accomplish remarkable things. These categories constitute areas of my life in which I always want to be growing because they lead to empowerment and wealth. This type of thinking and goal setting will get you started on becoming rich.

At the beginning of the fourth quarter of every year I update my annual goal sheet in writing for each of these categories. Then I determine (again, in writing) what systems, tasks, or actions I need to get in place before the year ends, so my goals will be accomplished in the upcoming year. I always do this as the fourth quarter begins, so I have three months to put systems in place and accomplish tasks before the start of the new year.

For example, since one of my repeated goals was to increase my real estate sales business by another ten transactions each year, I focus on getting the word out about my business. I know marketing is a path to success, so one year I added my own website and made sure it was up and running before the end of the year.

Below is an example of one of my annual goal sheets:

Health Goal
Start lifting weights three times per week.

Relationship Goal
Take my wife out to dinner every Friday night.

Education Goal
Attend one seminar and one conference every year and read one book per month.

Sales Goal
Increase real estate business by adding ten transactions this year.

Marketing Goal
Start using an email marketing platform instead of MS Outlook.

Experiencing Life Goal
Research fly-fishing in New Zealand.
Plan three vacations this year with my wife.

Hobby Goal
Take my dad fishing once a week.

Personal Finance Goal
Pay off all my credit cards.

Investment Goal
Purchase four more rental units this year.

Income Goal
Earn $10,000 per month.

If you want to change your life and become rich, then you must have clearly defined goals and make them your priority. Write your goals down and post them somewhere you can see them every day. Break down your goal into smaller goals and track your progress in writing on a score board. Imagine your new life when you accomplish your goal. Find a mentor who you trust and respect to hold you accountable for your progress in achieving the life of your dreams.

ASSET #2: PEOPLE

SURROUND YOURSELF WITH THE RIGHT PEOPLE

"Surround yourself with those who only lift you higher."
—Oprah Winfrey

Surrounding yourself with the right people is a cardinal rule for change and success. Those who are successful, happy, and rich live by this rule every day. When I started considering who I was surrounding myself with, I began to understand how to make the changes necessary in my social circle so that my happiness, success, and wealth could increase.

Let me back up. If you're not happy with your income, health, standard of living, employment, education level, net worth, or any other aspect of your life, you don't have to look further than the people you spend the most time with. Take a close look at these people. Are they doing better or worse than you in life? Many times, it's worse. This is sad for them but also worrisome for you. Your life right now is the direct result of the beliefs you have, the decisions you make, AND the people you spend time with. It's that simple.

If you surround yourself with friends who are going nowhere and do nothing but hang out on a barstool, drink, and complain about the economy, I guarantee it will drag you down. If your friends have nothing but problems and are always getting into trouble, sooner or later their problems will become your problems. Eventually you will be in trouble, too. If your friends are broke and bad with money, you will be broke, too. If your friends are cheating on their spouses or stealing from their employers, then they will lie and cheat on you and steal from you.

Let me illustrate this effect with a story from when I was a freshman in college. I became friends with a bunch of guys who were on the university's golf team. They were great guys and we had a blast together. Unfortunately, we had a little too much fun. We spent more time drinking and having fun than going to class and studying. I had a 0.6 grade point average after my freshman year. I was kicked out of school midway through my sophomore year.

After I was asked to leave college, I got a job with a construction company digging ditches and pushing wheelbarrows of concrete around. Talk about back breaking work! Fortunately for me, many of the kids I grew up with in my neighborhood were more studious than I and they were succeeding at college. They didn't get kicked out of school for partying. As my friends were growing up with their college experience, making new friends, and talking about their futures, I was not growing. My friends were surrounding themselves with other successful college students. I was working with a bunch of older guys who were suffering from bad backs due to lengthy careers in the construction industry. I was growing apart from my friends down the street from me, who I had known almost my entire life. I did not like this pattern. We just were not on the same page anymore, socially or intellectually. I was jealous of this growth they were experiencing, and I did not want to lose my friends. These close lifetime friends are what motivated me to cut out the partying and go back to college.

I applied and was accepted to the Rochester Institute of Technology. I graduated from RIT with a bachelor's degree in electrical engineering. It was a challenging program for me because I was never a good student. I always struggled to get good grades. When I went back to college, I was serious about getting my education and graduating.

To help me get good grades and make my life easier, I decided to observe what the smart kids were doing and try to emulate them. I perceived several traits of most of the smart students. They always sat up front, they never missed class, and they typically studied with other smart people. A great quote to use when you want to obtain or acquire what someone else has is this: *"Find someone who has what you want, do what they do, and you will get what they have."*

This quote worked perfectly for me when I was at RIT. I started sitting in the front row in every one of my classes. I never missed class, no matter what. Third and most importantly, I joined a study group with other students who were serious about meeting weekly to study and share solutions to all the homework problems. The results were incredible. I made the Dean's list that semester.

Your choice of people to live with, fall in love with, play with, work with, and invest with will be the most important decisions you will ever make. The people in your life that you spend time with have more impact on your chances of changing, growing, succeeding, being happy, and building wealth than any other factor.

If you want something different for yourself, then you need to start doing different things. This applies to the people you spend your time with. If you aren't willing to change your crowd, then you won't be able to change your income or net worth either. This is crucial to your success. However, let's be real—this is the category that will be the hardest to change. Later in the chapter, we'll discuss how to go about making these difficult changes.

Sports are a metaphor for life. Think about the most successful professional athletes. They are surrounded by the best coaches. They have stadiums full of raving fans, with professional cheerleaders cheering them on from the sidelines. They play in stadiums with comfortable locker rooms, state-of-the-art fitness centers, and professional rehab staff. You need to start living your life as though you are a professional athlete and ask yourself the following questions:

- Who is your coach?
- Where are your fans?
- Do you have cheerleaders?
- What is your stadium environment like?

It is critical to consider who you are letting into your life. One person can completely change your life. This works both ways. Just one great mentor can send you down the path for health and wealth that you could not have imagined! In the same way, one wrong toxic person can completely derail you. If you are truly serious about changing your life and becoming rich, then you must assess the people in your sphere of influence.

I spent the first half of my life surrounded by people who came to me by default. My first friends were the people who lived in my neighborhood. The other people who came to me by default were the members of my immediate family. None of us can change who our parents, siblings, or other relatives are. We have no choice about the family we've been born into. Your sphere of influence is a term used to describe all the people you spend the most time with. Most of us probably develop our sphere of influence simply through association by default. Most people enter our lives because we are related to them, we work with them, live next door to them or sit next to them at school.

If you think about it, for the first fifteen to twenty years of our lives, we meet people by default. It is completely random. The first people we all meet are our parents when we are born. Next, we meet our siblings and relatives. When we are old enough to go outside and play, we typically play with the kids next door or down the street. That is our only option if we want to make friends. On top of that, our parents tell us right before we go outside; "Don't talk to strangers". That is good advice when we are children but not so good for later in life. What happens when we start school? Typically, we get close to the kids in our classroom and especially who sits next to us. When we get our first job, we get to know all our fellow employees and the people sitting or working next to us.

My point here is that for the first fifteen to twenty years of our lives we are not taught to think about who we surround ourselves with. It is completely random and chosen for us. We haven't deliberately chosen to be around these people. This happens to all of us and it's okay. But if you want to change your life and become rich, going forward you must consider who you spend your time with and how they affect you. Once you start doing this, you'll really be able to step forward toward thinking and acting like a rich person.

I believe there are six basic types of people we can have in our lives.

1. Mentor/Coach
2. Team Member
3. Cheerleader
4. Neutral Person
5. Critic
6. Toxic Blocker

Who are Your Mentors and Coaches?

Finding a mentor or a coach should be your number one priority when you are changing who you surround yourself with. A mentor can be a person who has an exponential impact on your personal growth. They can truly help you change your life.

A mentor is a person who has a high level of expertise in their field or industry. This is someone who demonstrates ethical behavior and concern for others. This sort of person both gives back and pays it forward. Mentors have a teaching mentality and share what they know with others. They have a proven track record of success, as well as a positive attitude. Mentors help others believe in themselves.

Warren Buffett makes a good point about success: "It is okay to learn from mistakes, just make sure they are someone else's." Finding a good mentor is an effective way to learn from other's mistakes and successes. I have spent most of my life without mentors, learning everything through trial and error. As they say, I attended 'The School of Hard Knocks.' One of the main reasons I am writing this book is to share everything I have learned the hard way, so you don't have to go through the headaches and heartaches I have endured in my life.

As I told you before, I teamed up with my lifelong best friend in my first business partnership. After 12 years of doing business together, we realized we were never on the same page when it came to managing employees or money. When money got tight, we started fighting and our relationship came to an end. Unfortunately, I hadn't known anything at the time about creating legal partnership documents, which would have included a buy-sell agreement and a dissolution clause. This would have helped me immensely when we decided to go our separate ways. As it was, we had no structure in place and went through a nasty business breakup. Miserable, I spent a lot of money and lost a lot of sleep for three straight years.

If I had a mentor when I'd gone into business with my friend, my mentor would have guided me through the business decisions I needed to make, both at the beginning of my business and as I navigated through the murky legal waters. I was flying blind and had no idea what I was doing. I ended up losing money, time, and my best friend. This was an expensive and painful lesson for me.

A good mentor would have encouraged me to surround myself with a business team of professionals like an attorney, insurance agent, real estate agent, accountant, banker/loan officer, and financial planner. Having trusted professionals like this would have ensured my ventures were successful and that I was protected as an individual.

These key professionals would have mentored me in their areas of expertise and kept me from the problems I faced. They also can prevent people from losing money, getting sued, or having problems with the IRS.

A good mentor can do so many positive things for you. One good mentor can literally change the course of your life. The following is a list of some of the ways a mentor can have a positive impact on your life:

- Save you from trial and error and learning things the hard way.
- Fast track your expertise in a certain area of life or business.
- Provide motivation and hold you accountable.
- Loan money to you to start your business or purchase an investment.
- Help you find private lenders.
- Help you with strategic decisions, planning, and goal setting.
- Help you find investment deals.
- Introduce you to other mentors.
- Suggest educational resources, seminars, books, etc.

So how do you find this trusted mentor? Ask a successful friend, relative, coworker, boss, or neighbor. People you already know are usually willing to help you. Another idea is to join a club. If you're interested in real estate investing, you could join your local landlord association. Or you could take part in an investment club. How about joining a service organization like Rotary International or Kiwanis? You could join your local Chamber of Commerce, which often holds networking events that could help you find the trusted mentor of your dreams. Business Networking International and Toastmasters are both great organizations to surround yourself with successful people. Not only are clubs a fun place to meet people who have the same ideas, motivations, or goals you have, but they can also be an excellent place to find a mentor.

If you want to surround yourself with like-minded people who are trying to build wealth and become rich, then joining an organization is something to consider. Chances are most of the members have had a mentor at one time in their life. Usually they are willing to return the favor by helping someone like you. When it comes to success and becoming rich, you don't need to reinvent the wheel. You can avoid a lot of mistakes by learning from these people. Go find where the rich people and investors are meeting and gain access to that group of people.

If you like to golf, then become a caddy at the country club in your region. Successful high-net-worth people like to golf. If you don't golf, then get a job cleaning the locker rooms or waiting tables—just get in the door of the club. Get a job at the local yacht club performing a service for sailboat owners. People who own sailboats are typically well off. Find a job at the tennis club. People who can afford to play tennis at a club are typically successful investors, high-paid professionals and business owners. Do whatever it takes to get your foot in the door. Clean the floors if that is what it takes to get access to these potential mentors.

Read your local newspaper and see who is making headlines. Figure out who is making waves in the way you'd like to make waves. If you're interested in becoming a real estate investor like me, find out who's purchasing property in the region. Who is involved in development projects?

If you are intimidated by reaching out to someone

you don't know, then try the approach I use every day. This approach is one of the best ways to find a mentor to help you become rich. It is free and available to anyone who wants to use it. It is open 24 hours a day and never denies you access. It is called the Internet. Today, there is more information flowing freely across the Internet than ever before. Entire libraries of data and educational materials are waiting for you. Podcasts, YouTube videos, and online blogs and articles burst with information on how to change your life and build wealth. Stop watching shows like Lost, Breaking Bad, The Originals, and Game of Thrones and get serious about educating yourself so you can become rich. Below is a list of people who produce my favorite Podcasts or YouTube videos or have written life-changing books. I consider these people to be my mentors:

- Patrick Bet-David (Valuetainment)
- Tom Bilyeu (Impact Theory)
- Eric Thomas
- Earl Nightingale
- Jim Rohn
- Les Brown
- Tony Robbins
- Zig Ziglar
- Pat Flynn (Smart Passive Income)
- Tim Ferriss
- Gary Vaynerchuk (Ask GaryV show)
- Tai Lopez
- Justin Perry (http://youarecreators.org)

When you're looking for a potential mentor, ask yourself a couple questions. First, is the person ethical? Make sure you select a mentor who is honest and can be trusted. If they are not fair and honest with other people, then they won't be honest with you. You need to have a very high level of trust with your mentor.

Does the mentor you have in mind have a positive, happy attitude? You want to be spending time with a mentor who is happy and positive because one of the benefits of having a mentor is that they will motivate you to succeed. If a person has a negative attitude and they are always complaining and criticizing other people, then chances are they won't be a good mentor.

It's also quite important to make sure the potential mentor has experience and success in the field or industry you want to pursue. If you are trying to build wealth, you can't take advice from a person standing in the unemployment line. You need to find people who are successful at building wealth if you want to become successful at building wealth. In the same way, if you want to become a bodybuilder, then join a gym where all the best competitive bodybuilders go. If you show up every day and ask them for advice, you'll learn their strategy. The most important thing is to find a mentor who has already succeeded at whatever it is you want to acquire in life.

When it comes to selecting a mentor, you want to play up in life! When you ski behind a good skier, you start to ski better. When you play tennis with better tennis players, you start playing better tennis. When you hang out with investors, entrepreneurs, and happy successful people, your life will change for the better—you will think, act, and make decisions like these successful mentors.

How do you approach a mentor? The simplest way to recruit a mentor is simply to ask them if they will mentor you. One of the most basic needs of people is to feel important. When we ask another person for help, they feel important. If you ask another person to mentor you, chances are they will feel complimented by your request and might agree to help you. You should still be ready to offer something in return for their help. The right mentor will have a great attitude and enjoy helping other people. They might agree to mentor you just because they'd enjoy the challenge of helping someone less fortunate.

However, be ready for all types of responses. It might go something like this: "Why should I mentor you? What are you going to do for me?" If Warren Buffett or Bill Gates called me tomorrow and asked me to work for them for an entire year for free and in exchange, they would mentor me, I would drop what I am doing and go running! That would be an opportunity of a lifetime. You need to be prepared to offer something in return for your mentor's guidance and expertise.

If you find a great mentor and they want you to do something in return for mentoring services, I suggest you offer anything you can that is legal and ethical to become their student. Offer to be their personal assistant, marketing person, landscaper, or house cleaner. Offer to do research for their company or latest business idea. Offer to wash and wax their car for a year. I'm not kidding! How bad do you want a great mentor? If you find a truly great mentor, they can alter your future in so many great ways that cleaning their car or house for free for a year will be a drop in the bucket compared to what they are going to do for you. Remember, they don't need you—*you need them!*

Another way to find a mentor is to hire one. Before you dismiss this idea of paying another person to help you become rich, consider that we pay for other kinds of lessons. We pay for tennis, music, driving, or swimming lessons. Why is it when it comes to one of the most important aspects of our future—money—we don't invest in any education? I will never understand that. Rich people hire the best and most expensive accountants, tax consultants, and investment advisors because they know they are investing in their net worth and financial freedom.

Every year Warren Buffett auctions off a one-hour lunch with himself for charity. In 2017, an anonymous bidder paid $2.68 million dollars for that lunch date. I doubt if lunch with any human being is worth that much money, but I think you get the point. Rich people will pay other rich people for advice and coaching.

According to Tony Robbins, "If you want to be successful, find someone who has achieved the results you want and copy what they do, and you'll achieve the same results."

You Need Team Members to Succeed

Another person who comes into your life is a team member. These folks want to see you succeed and are willing to act and invest their time and money in your mission and dreams. Team members can provide valuable resources that can be the difference between success and failure.

A team member might be a spouse, sibling, parent, relative, friend, coworker, or employer. They can provide a place to live, advice, motivation, financial support, or money. They might not be a mentor, but they could possibly know and introduce you to someone else who could be a mentor.

One of my best friends, Ray, moved to York, PA, to live with his uncle while he started a car detailing business. Ray's uncle put a roof over his head while he got his new business venture off the ground. Twenty years later, Ray is a multi-millionaire with several car dealerships and a cash-flowing rental property portfolio. I would say that his uncle was one of Ray's early team members who helped him on his road to success.

In my own life, I've enjoyed having team members. For instance, I was able to purchase several profitable rental properties with money friends and colleagues (a.k.a. team members) loaned me. I would not have been able to make those acquisitions without the help of these people who believed in me and wanted to help me.

Don't forget the people who help you and try to return the favor someday. If they loan you money, always pay it back, no matter what the circumstances. Under no circumstances should you burn a bridge with a team member.

Cheerleaders Keep us Motivated and Support Us

Another sort of person who can help you is the cheerleader. This is a person who may not have the resources to be a team member, but they want you to succeed just the same. A cheerleader can be a spouse, sibling, parent, relative, friend, coworker, or employer. Your mentor and team members will also be some of your best cheerleaders! The other people I mentioned will be more readily available than your mentor, so you need both sources of cheerleading.

Emotional support is very helpful when you're trying to make changes in your life. Some people will always doubt you, so that's why it's important to counter that with positive energy and support from your cheerleaders, who want you to succeed. Cheerleaders will be happy for you if you reach your goals. There will always be times when you need someone to tell you that you are doing the right thing and not to quit when the going gets rough.

Neutral People Exist in all our Lives

Neutral people are just that: neutral. They aren't mentors, team members, or cheerleaders. They are not detractors either. Neutral people are typically siblings, parents, or spouses. They don't say much when you tell them you plan on changing your life to become successful and rich. These folks don't weigh in one way or the other. Telling them about your plans really doesn't matter to them. They are neither negative nor positive about your goals. Don't try to force a neutral person to be a mentor, team member, or cheerleader. Neutral people are usually neutral because they don't want to be involved due to their own fears or they don't want to take any risks. When it comes to neutral people, let sleeping dogs lie.

Ignore the Critics

Unfortunately, the world is full of critics. These are the people who will doubt you and, more than likely, you know many of them. The closest people to you are usually some of your biggest critics. They will be your spouse, siblings, parents, relatives, friends, coworkers, or employers. Critics don't stand in your way, but they will take every opportunity they can to tell you how you are making a mistake, wasting your time, and you aren't capable. They might even share your goals and plans in a negative way to other people or on social media. Be prepared for their criticism and negative talk.

Some classic statements from critics might be:

- You aren't smart enough!

- You weren't born rich and you never will be!
- You are going to lose your money!
- Oh, now you think you are too *good* for us!
- You are selling out!
- Those new friends of yours are just using you!

Critics will put you down for two reasons. They are afraid for you and this is their way of trying to stop you from what they think is a bad idea. The second reason is they are jealous you are doing something they don't have the confidence to try themselves.

Either way, you have several choices when it comes to handling critics. You can tell them to stop with the criticism and get behind you and become a cheerleader. The second choice is to ask them to say nothing at all and be a neutral person. The third choice is to remove the critic from your life and not spend any time around them. This can be a difficult choice to make if the critic is someone close to you. But, if their criticism is holding you down, it might be time to let them go so you can fly to your dreams.

Do not allow a critic to linger in your life because you are afraid to confront this person. One critic can have a constant negative effect on you and become a dream killer.

Avoid Toxic Blockers

Toxic blockers lead toxic lives and surround themselves with other toxic people. These people get into trouble, live unethical lives, and even break the law. They typically abuse substances like drugs and alcohol. Toxic blockers tend to be confrontational and even violent. They make themselves feel good by making other people feel bad. They will go out of their way to hold you back or set you up for failure. They might even be abusing you emotionally, physically, or socially. You can't trust these people and you must completely and permanently remove them from your life.

It is unlikely you will be able to change a toxic blocker. If you associate with someone like this, you must get serious about inviting them out of your life. If it is your spouse, sibling, or parent, you will have an extremely difficult decision to make. It is almost impossible to change your life if you are spending any time around a toxic blocker. They will set you up for failure every chance they get. This will never change. You cannot become rich with a toxic blocker in your life.

The Influencers in Your Life

Motivational speaker Jim Rohn famously said that we are the average of the five people we spend the most time with. I believe this statement is very true when it comes to all aspects of our lives. In the same way, our happiness, health, and wealth will be the average of the people we spend most of our time with as well. Below is a list of the kinds of people you more than likely spend most of your time with. Because of this, these will be the most influential people in your life.

- Your partner/spouse.
- Your boss/coworkers.
- Your parents, siblings, and relatives.
- Your friends.

Partner/Spouse

When it comes to deciding who your life partner is, you don't have to look any further than that person's relationship with their siblings and the quality of their parents' marriage.

If their relationship with their siblings is adversarial, confrontational, or contentious, then their relationship with you is going to be the same. If they act a certain way with their own flesh and blood, then it's likely they aren't going to treat you any better. Make sure the person you choose to partner with or marry is a person who loves and trusts their siblings and wants to be around their family.

Our family history and the environment we grow up in have an impact on how we live, play, and work with other people. We are the products of our environment. Our compatibility level, communication skills, conflict resolution skills, and positive or negative attitude is hereditary. I do believe these personal attributes can be worked on and improved but you are taking a big chance if you think you are going to change someone.

Also, it's important to choose your life partner very wisely. This person is someone you'll be spending most of your time with. If your romantic partner can't manage their money, then eventually you'll be sharing their debts, and they will be wasting your money too. In the same way, if your life partner doesn't take care of their health, you'll either become their personal nurse or you'll be financially impacted by their health care costs. Or worse, you'll take on their exercise and diet habits and feel physically poor yourself. Your life partner can be a profound impact on your future.

Boss/Coworkers

Is your boss or your employer helping you grow?

Make sure your boss is your biggest cheerleader. He or she should be a mentor and always willing to help you do better. It's best to work for people who want you to succeed.

This might sound obvious but there are many supervisors out there who only want you to be just good enough to get your work done. They don't want their staff members to do too well because it might make them look bad. They also don't want you to grow as an employee because you might be considered for a promotion before them. Many supervisors are where they are at because of the Peter Principle: they have risen to the level of their incompetence. These bosses will always set you up for failure.

The same concept applies to your coworkers. Try to find people you work with who are engaged in their jobs and the work that they do. There are so many people today who act like they hate their jobs and it shows. They sit around bashing the company and their boss every chance they get. Stay away from these people. They are bad for you and give off a ton of negative energy. Stay clear of the complainers. There are great benefits to socializing with coworkers who have a positive attitude and want to make a difference and who care about the quality of their work. First off, you will learn more about the company's business processes, possible job openings, new job skills, etc. Second, you will have a positive image in the eyes of the people who own or run the company. Third, if there is a downturn in business and the company needs to lay people off, I can assure you the employees who do all the complaining are always the first to go.

Aim to work for a company and a boss that want you to grow and succeed. Find a company with growth opportunities that provides training and educational benefits. Once you're there, hang around with those coworkers who are most positive and happy to help you live your best life. You might have to change jobs if you determine that your boss, company, or coworkers are having a harmful effect on your life or your attitude.

Parents, Siblings, and Relatives

This is one of the toughest groups of people to analyze and change because we are born into this circle of people and we cannot change it no matter what we do. Another reason this is such a critical group of people is because regardless of how much time we spend with them, their thoughts, comments, and opinions have a big effect on us.

Unfortunately, the people related to us can be the most negative about our goals and dreams. They are often the ones who warn us against taking any chances. They might tell us we'll lose all our money or that we're not smart enough to accomplish anything. If they aren't 100% behind you, don't discuss your dreams with them. Make sure that when you're sharing your plans with loved ones, they're supportive. If they won't help you or at least be your cheerleader, then keep them out of the loop. They need to be happy for you—not jealous or negative.

If you trust these people, then ask them to be cheerleaders, team members, or mentors to you. If you already fear what they will say, and you don't trust them, then keep your goals and dreams to yourself. Minimize the time you spend with them and the information you share with them. If you feel you must tell them about your goals and plans, then only share information after it has been accomplished or completed. If you plan on attending a seminar on starting an online business, only share this information after you attend the seminar or start your new business. This way they can't talk you out of it with negative comments.

Friends

This is another tough group of people to analyze and change because we have typically known our friends for a long time.

If you trust your friends, then ask them to be cheerleaders, team members, or mentors. Just as with your family if you fear what they will say, and you don't trust them, then keep your goals and dreams to yourself. Minimize the time you spend with them and the information you share with them. If you feel you must tell them about your goals and plans, then again, only share parts of your life after the fact. If you don't trust your friends enough for them to be cheerleaders or a team member, then it might be time to get some new friends. You can always make new friends.

As I've said before, if you want to change your life, you're going to need to analyze and possibly change many aspects of what you're currently doing. Finding friends who have a positive influence on you is a good place to start. This might sound like a hardened view, but if you feel you need to change your life in a significant way, then you should consider if the friends you're spending time with are good for you.

How to Analyze Your Influencers

It is important for you to take some time to think about who your influencers are. Make a list of the people you spend the most time with. It can be family members, relatives, friends, or coworkers. It doesn't necessarily have to be five people. It can be three people, or it can be ten people. The key here is to determine who you are spending the most time with. This is the list of people who are going to help you or hurt you on the path to your dreams. You must know who they are and then analyze their effect on you.

Earlier, we discussed the roles various people play in your life. They can be mentors, team members, cheerleaders, neutral influences, critics, or toxic blockers. Here's a short exercise for you. Write down the names of the people who you think are influencers and next to their name, write down the role each of these people currently play in your life. In another column, write down what role you wished they would play for you.

Your list should look like this:

NAME	CURRENT ROLE	FUTURE ROLE
James	Cheerleader	Team member
Janet	Critic	Neutral Person
Raymond	Neutral Person	Cheerleader
Beth	Team Member	Team Member
Jim	Team Member	Team Member
Sarah	Neutral Person	Cheerleader
Sally	Critic	Neutral Person
Bill	Toxic Blocker	Avoid or Remove

Make sure everyone in the list above is a person you spend a lot of time around or a person whose comments or opinions have a big effect on you. The reason they are on the list is because they have a strong impact on you, in one way or another. Because these are the people who have the biggest influence on your life, they also impact your chances of changing and becoming rich.

In analyzing these people, consider whether there's anything you can do to improve the role they play for you in your life. If the person is good for you, then maintain the relationship as it is. If the person is harmful for you, can you encourage them to be more helpful to you in some way? If not, consider minimizing the time you spend with them or even removing them permanently from your life. Tim Ferriss, an American entrepreneur, author, and podcaster said this: *"A person's success in life can usually be measured by the number of uncomfortable conversations he or she is willing to have."* You might have to conduct some uncomfortable conversations to improve or remove the influence of the people in your life.

Consider this analogy. The winner of a bass fishing tournament is the boat that catches six fish with the heaviest combined weight. For example, if your boat catches six bass weighing one pound each, then your combined weight at the end of the tournament is six pounds. If you were to catch six fish weighing in two pounds each, then your combined weight is twelve pounds.

At the start of the fishing contest, the anglers try to catch any six fish they can as soon as possible. After they have six fish, their goal then switches to increasing the total weight of their six fish. When they catch a seventh fish, if it weighs more than any of the six fish they currently have, they release the lightest fish they're currently holding in the live well of their boat and keep the new one they just caught. This increases the total weight of their six fish. As the day goes on, they continue to replace light fish with heavier fish.

You might be asking yourself what this has to do with the people in your life. What I'm suggesting is that you might have to "throwback" some people if they are hurting you and not making positive contributions to your goal of changing your life. The goal is to replace the people who are hurting you or holding you back with new people who want to help you. People are a huge Life Asset in your life, and they can help you do incredible things. Unfortunately, they also have the power to hurt you tremendously.

Always try to motivate the people in your life to be cheerleaders, team members, or even mentors if they have mentor qualifications. If someone is a critic, then get them to be neutral or get them out of your life. Most toxic blockers will not change, so be prepared to get them out of your life at all costs.

When it comes to letting people into your life, you need to adopt the mindset of an employer. If you owned your own company or small business, you would not hire the first person who walks through your door. You wouldn't hire your neighbor just because he or she lives next door to you. You might not even hire your best friend unless they met your qualifications. Employers spend billions of dollars every year on human resource departments, human resource professionals, software, and candidate screening processes. They want the most talented staff so their company can succeed, grow, and be profitable.

You need to take the same time and care when you decide who you want to let into your life. Your life is like a business and your friends, family, co-workers, employer, and mentor are like your employees. They can make or break you. This approach to deciding who you spend time with might sound cold and calculated. That's because it is very calculated, and you need to remove your feelings and emotions and just use logic. It's up to you if you want to change or stay the same. You can't change your life unless you change the people in it.

Below is a list of questions to ask about the people who have the power to influence you in your life and what kind of effect they are having on your chances for change and success.

FINANCIAL questions to ask yourself about each person on your list:

- What is their annual salary?
- Do they own any assets like real estate, stocks or a business?
- What is their net worth?
- What are their financial liabilities?
- How much money have they saved over the past year?
- What is their plan for retirement?
- What is their debt level and credit score?
- Have they ever been foreclosed on or claimed bankruptcy?

GROWTH questions to ask yourself about each person on your list:

- What is their education level?
- What is the title of the latest book they read?
- How do they spend their free time?
- Do they have any goals?
- What is their current employment status?
- How long have they been at the same job without a promotion?

PERSONAL questions to ask yourself about each

person on your list:

- Have they ever been arrested?
- What are they like when they have been drinking?
- Do they drink too much or too often?
- Have they ever cheated on their spouse?
- How do they treat their children, spouse, siblings, parents, or friends?
- How do they talk about their children, spouse, siblings, parents, and friends?
- What is their health like?
- Would you be afraid to share your goals and dreams with this person?
- What will this person tell you when the going gets rough or when you start to fail?
- Do they complain a lot?
- When they find out about your goal of becoming rich, what will they say?
- If you asked them for help, would they offer it?
- As you make the changes in your life and move toward becoming rich, how will they feel if you succeed?

This is a tough set of questions to ask. You might love the people on your list and truly enjoy the time you spend with them, but the people you surround yourself with will have to change if you want to become rich. This is not negotiable. The people you spend time with have a direct impact on your net worth and income. If you are not currently rich, then you are hanging out with the wrong people.

The Chain of Events

When you surround yourself with successful people, it has a multiplying effect. One good thing leads to another. When good things happen, usually even more good things happen. You gain momentum when you are around the right people. This philosophy is part of the theory that the rich get richer and it takes money to make money. I truly believe that you must surround yourself with good people if you want good things to happen. If you hang around successful people, then success will follow. There is an inevitable chain of events that occurs from your association with each person in your life. It is either a positive chain of events or a negative chain of events.

Babel, a movie starring Brad Pitt, is about how one decision a person makes sets in motion a chain of events that can affect another person on the other side of the world. This premise is so true when it comes to surrounding yourself with the right people. Being around another successful person can expose you to a concept, a piece of knowledge, a new method to perform, a task, an important lead, or a great investment opportunity that can have an exponential impact on improving the quality of your life.

In the summer of 2006, I found myself taking a cruise on a 50-foot yacht at our local yacht club. The owner of the yacht is a very successful and well-known business owner and entrepreneur. The other passengers on the yacht were all very accomplished as well. I felt very fortunate to be in the company of such a successful group of people. I just sat there while the owner of the boat and a local multi-millionaire real estate developer talked about some major developments taking place in the local region. I was giddy inside; I was getting access to this kind of information just because I happened to be on the boat that night! As I sat there on that million-dollar vessel taking in a perfect evening (and eating prime rib!), I asked myself how I got there. I could not afford to join the yacht club let alone own a 50-foot yacht. I wound up in that very desirable situation because of the conscious decision to surround myself with successful people. It was a chain of events that was the result of getting to know one successful person.

The very first real estate office I worked in had a senior real estate agent named Bill. Before I became a real estate sales agent, my business partners and I had a building we wanted to sell. I called Bill because I'd seen his name on so many For Sale signs on buildings in the area. Since it looked like this man was a successful realtor, I called him for his opinion about our building.

I gave him a complete set of information about our building and asked him to get back to me with a suggested price. A week later Bill called me and said the information I gave him was very impressive and I should consider becoming a real estate agent myself. This suggestion set in motion a chain of events that has culminated with me owning my own real estate brokerage and becoming the president of my local Rotary Club, accomplishments I'm very proud of. This entire chain of events happened all because I met Bill.

I can recall numerous other lucrative events that have occurred because I chose to accept a position as a real estate agent at Bill's office. Bill worked in the headquarters of the real estate franchise where the owner of the franchise and his very wealthy business partner also worked. I was looking for a new opportunity and a new career choice.

When Bill asked me to come into his office to see what they did, I accepted his invitation. When I arrived, I saw some impressive cars in the parking lot: an Audi, a Mercedes-Benz, a BMW, and a Lexus! Everyone inside was well-dressed and photos of all the commercial property the brokerage owned decorated the walls. It didn't take long for me to realize that this was a place where I could surround myself with successful people. I knew if I worked hard some crumbs would fall off the table, and I could pick them up.

To say I picked up a lot of crumbs during the time I spent working at Bill's office is an understatement. It is amazing how just one successful person can set off such a dramatic, positive chain of events in your life. Unfortunately, the same can be said for a long-term association with one wrong, negative person. Surrounding yourself with successful people really pays off.

Other Ways to Surround Yourself With the Right People

ATTEND SEMINARS AND CONFERENCES

Today you can find a seminar for any goal, business idea, or industry you want to pursue. People who attend seminars and conferences are excited about changing their lives. These are the people you want to be around. Their positive and forward thinking is contagious, and it will rub off on you, motivating you to climb to new heights. These events have speakers who are already successful at what you want to accomplish. They give talks and sell products to help you reach your goals. You will make connections with these people, forging relationships that will have a positive impact on your goals and life.

JOIN BUSINESS AND INVESTMENT CLUBS

Join your local landlord and investment club if you want to become a stock or real estate investor. The resources at these clubs are fabulous and the people there are typically happy to help new investors. These clubs have regular meetings with guest speakers, and they have educational programs to help you get started.

JOIN A SERVICE ORGANIZATION

Join your local Rotary or Kiwanis club. These are humanitarian clubs that give back to the community. Their members are typically business owners and investors. These are great people to surround yourself with, since they typically have successful, positive attitudes. These clubs are a good place to find a mentor.

JOIN A NETWORKING GROUP

BNI (Business Networking International) is a good example of a networking group. You must pay to join, but you get to be around business owners and professionals who are trying to grow their business and income. If you ask around, you might be able to find other, less formal networking clubs with professionals in your area. Again, the members of this type of club are good people to know. They can be helpful and inspirational for you on your path to success.

ASSET #3: TIME

VALUE YOUR TIME

"You cannot save time, find time or make time.
You can only stop wasting time."
—Joe Herbert

Every person possesses different amounts or levels of the six Life Assets, except time. Time is the only Life Asset we all get the same amount of and that never changes. Everyone is given the same amount of time each day. The richest person in the world and the poorest person in the world are both given twenty-four hours a day. One of the big differences between successful people and unsuccessful people is what they do with their time. Rich people use their time to make money, self-educate, improve their lives, have fun, and help other people. How we decide to use our time is one of the major factors that will determine if you can change your life and become rich.

An important concept about time is that we cannot make, find or save time. If you can figure out how to do any of that, you will become the richest person in the world overnight. The only thing you can do is avoid wasting time. How many times have you heard the following statements: "I need to make time for that," "I just can't find the time," or "If you do it this way you can save some time?"

Unfortunately, most people do not value their time because it is free. We get twenty-four hours for free at the start of every day whether we ask for it or not. The movie "In Time" starring Justin Timberlake, is a great example of what would happen if time were not free and each person had a limited supply. The movie is about a future where people stop aging at 25. The downside is they only live one more year after that. If a person wants to live longer, they must barter and pay for more time. Time became the new currency. I'm not saying you must value time like this, but you must change how you view time and what do each day with your 24 hours, if you want to become rich.

Do not be a philanthropist with time and money if you aren't rich. You must take care of yourself first. What does the flight attendant on a Jet airplane tell everyone right before take-off? "In the event of an emergency, put your oxygen mask on first then help the person sitting next to you." The same principle should be observed with your time. If you are not where you want to be in achieving your goals, then you should use your time to become rich first before you give your time to anyone else.

Whatever you spend a lot of time doing, that is what you will be good at. This statement may seem obvious, but it is one of the most overlooked rules when it comes to changing your life and becoming rich. Human beings are creatures of habit. As we get older, we settle into a life of redundancy and habit. Most people do not like stepping outside their comfort zone, so they do the same things over and over. We stay at the same job. We socialize with the same people. We eat the same foods, we watch and listen to the same internet and TV content, listen to the same music, and go to the same restaurants. If you are not rich and you want to become rich, then you must be willing to change almost everything about your life, especially what you do with your time. If you are not rich, it is because you are spending too much time not acting rich.

If you spend a lot of time lifting weights, then you will develop strong muscles. I used to go to a gym that had a lot of serious bodybuilders. It didn't matter when I went there, the guys with the biggest muscles were always there. They were there when I arrived, and they were still there when I left. It was no wonder these guys had great bodies. Their entire diet focused on eating lots of calories and protein. All they thought about was getting big. All their friends were bodybuilders too. Consequently, they got bigger because they spent a lot of time trying to build muscle. I don't know what their bank accounts looked like, but they were buff.

Warren Buffet is a stock investor who is worth billions of dollars. He didn't get lucky and pick some incredible stock that made him rich overnight. He started studying bond charts and stock market data when he was a young boy. He didn't make his first billion dollars until he was in his mid-fifties. Warren Buffet's life has revolved around the stock market and that is why he is rich. Bill Gates quit college and started Microsoft in his garage. He said he worked the first twenty-one years before he took a vacation.

These guys spent a lot of time perfecting their skills and companies; that is why they became good at it. They did not get lucky. Their success was not handed to them. They put in the hours over the years. They spend a lot of time being good at making money in the stock market and selling software.

This is a very simple concept, and it works at all levels of life. It works at the micro level with a job skill or athletic endeavor and it works at the macro level with your health and wealth. If you practice the habits of poor people over and over, then you will mostly likely remain poor. Just wanting and wishing to be rich will not change anything. You need to start using your time doing the things rich people do.

The basic premise of this book is how to act, think and believe like a rich person. The more time you spend acting rich the more likely it is you will become rich. It sounds simple, but making the changes in your life to act, think and believe like a rich person is not easy to do. The essential truth is this: Whatever you spend a lot of time doing, that is what you'll be good at.

Where does all the time go?

If you're like most people, your life is already busy with work, school, family, kids, and taking time out to have fun. You are probably asking yourself how you will be able to fit anything else in your busy schedule so you can start changing your life. We can't create, save or find more time - we only get 24 hours! The goal and challenge are to change what you already do with your time.

Let's start by analyzing what most of us are already doing with our time. It's essential for each of us to figure out how much time we're spending in each category and consider which activities contribute to our success, happiness, and health—and which of them do not. Then we will discuss what can be changed, what can be eliminated, and how to use leverage to get more done.

The following list is a breakdown of the main

categories of how people could use their time.

- Sleeping
- Eating
- Working for money
- Hygiene and health
- Unexpected interruptions, emergencies and accidents
- Unavoidable time wasters
- Life maintenance
- Socializing and entertainment
- Avoidable time wasters
- Self-education
- Creating passive income and building wealth

Sleeping

There are no subcategories for sleep. I put sleep in its own category because it is easy to measure how much time we spend sleeping. Sleep is not negotiable when you are trying to free up time to change your life. You can't ask someone to share their sleep with you, loan you some sleep or sleep on your behalf. There is no way to incorporate leverage here. You must perform this action on your own with your own time. I don't recommend sleeping less so you can free up time. Sleep is important for good health, motivation and focus.

But if you can't sleep, don't fight it. Get up and read, watch YouTube, or work on your business. Sometimes when I can't sleep, it's because I'm anxious about work, money, or investments. When I get up and journal about what is bothering me or take notes on how I will rectify the problem, my mind feels easier and I can go back to sleep.

Eating

Eating is another category that is non-negotiable. If you stop eating, you will get sick. I recommend that you continue to eat but take the time to eat good healthy food. Time can be saved in this category if you eat nothing but fast food. I don't recommend this for numerous reasons. Later in this book I will discuss how eating healthy can impact your chances of becoming rich. I have days when I am jammed up with tons of appointments or I am running late so I run through a drive through for a sandwich, but this only happens once or twice per month. I try to eat food that improves my health and allows me to perform at peak levels. Food matters when you are trying to become rich. Healthy food is fuel for success.

Acquiring and preparing food is an interesting subject today with all the online business startups dealing with food preparation and delivery. These online businesses offer versatile, reliable, and healthy choices. If you consider how fast, predictable, and reliable the logistics of shipping have become, having your food delivered to your home is a great option for freeing up time.

Working for money

Whether you work for an employer or you are self-employed, you'll most likely be spending at least 40 hours per week generating earned income. There's not much most of us can do to free up time here, at least until we build our passive income enough to no longer be dependent on a job.

Hygiene and health

Hygiene and health are somewhat like sleep in that you can't ask someone to do this for you. Hygiene and health are not mandatory like sleep, but I highly recommend you don't cut these activities out of your life to free up time for becoming rich. You can stop taking showers, shaving, brushing your teeth and working out, but I don't recommend it. You can ignore the chest pains you have been experiencing and skip the doctor's appointment, but you will probably keel over and be taken to the hospital.

Unexpected interruptions, emergencies and accidents

Unexpected interruptions, emergencies and accidents are a fact of life. Sometimes we can minimize the amount of time these events take and the impact they have on our lives, but these things are going to happen to us all. Poor people and rich people will experience these events. Call it fate or karma, but life's unexpected events do not favor or discriminate against or avoid any of us.

Everyone gets in car accidents, locked out of the house or car on occasion. Anyone can come down with a bad cold or the flu. We all lose loved ones sooner or later. When a natural disaster or extreme weather strikes, it impacts everyone.

Successful people have contingency plans in place to minimize the impact these events have on their lives. The goal of these plans is to reduce the financial and time loss incurred when these events do happen.

To help reduce the inconvenience of getting locked out of your house, have a Realtor's lockbox somewhere on the exterior of your house with a spare key in it. I lock myself out of my house at least five times a year. Can you imagine if I had to call my wife to come from work to let me in the house every time? What a huge waste of time!

The same thinking should be applied to handling being locked out of your car. Join AAA or subscribe to your car manufacturers cloud-based emergency service.

When it comes to losing loved ones, make sure you have life insurance for your immediate family so they can pay outstanding bills and funeral costs if you should lose a loved one in your household.

You won't get any speeding tickets if you don't speed. That one is simple and easy. Please do not drive drunk or drive and text under any circumstances. Some unexpected events can be completely avoided if you use your head. Your goal is to change and move forward in life. If you lose your driver's license, this will be a big mistake and set you back financially and socially. You will waste a lot of time if you can't drive.

There is nothing you can do to avoid having your car or home robbed. Hopefully, this never happens to you, but criminals don't discriminate. Robbery is a random act and it can happen to anyone. Make sure you have the proper insurances. Also, be sure to back up or save your computer data to the cloud. I never save any file on the hard drive of my computer. Everything I create and save on my computer is in Dropbox, Microsoft OneDrive or Google Drive. Make sure your phone and computer are password-protected. I save my contacts to Google contacts so if my phone is stolen or dropped in the water, I just buy a new phone and I am back in business in minutes.

Never leave your cell phone in an unprotected mode. Change the phone settings so it goes to password-protected mode after a few minutes of inactivity. Have the emergency phone numbers for your bank and credit card companies available and easy to find in case your bank account or credit cards are stolen or compromised.

Unavoidable Time Wasters

Waiting for something to happen, traveling some place and or communicating with people are unavoidable facts of life. I call these unavoidable time wasters because all too often we spend too much time doing them or they can be eliminated in many cases. The good news is there are ways to reduce the time used or wasted for these events by reducing the number of times you perform them or by multi-tasking during the event. Examples of things we might not be able to avoid include:

- Waiting in a reception area for a doctor, hospital visit or other professional service
- Getting stuck in traffic
- Waiting for your car to be fixed or maintained
- Sitting in the jury duty selection area
- Waiting for a home delivery or a utility company service person to show up
- Waiting to board a plane, bus, train, or boat
- Riding on a plane, bus, train, or boat
- Driving in your car
- Talking on the phone
- Responding to texts and emails
- Talking and socializing with your neighbor in your driveway for an hour
- Waiting for a friend to show up
- Waiting for your spouse to get ready

A few years ago, I received a summons letter for jury duty. I had to report to a room at the County courthouse and sit around for eight hours while they decided who they were going to select. There were at least a hundred people waiting. It amazed me how many of the people in the room completely wasted the entire day just sitting there doing nothing while they were waiting. Ironically, many of them were complaining to each other about how this was a huge waste of their time. They didn't realize it, but they were the people responsible for wasting their own time. In the entire room there was only one girl who had brought a book with her. I brought my computer because at that time I was writing Get Rich in 5 Hours, and I wanted to take advantage of the time I was there. This might sound crazy, but I was looking forward to being locked in the room waiting because I hadn't worked on my book for a couple of weeks. I was excited to have some dedicated time to make progress. I'm becoming richer every day because this is how I think, plan and use my time. I think like a rich person and I value my time.

In February of 2018 I took a fly-fishing trip to a tiny island south of Honolulu. The island was named Kiritimati. At that time, I was living in Erie, which is in the very northwest corner of Pennsylvania. This little island is so far from my hometown it might as well have been on the moon. The flight from my hometown to Honolulu alone took eleven hours. The second leg of the trip was a four-hour flight from Honolulu to Kiritimati. I was looking forward to the flight time because I wanted to work on this book. I made sure I had all my files for this book loaded on my computer hard drive in case I did not have inflight Wi-Fi internet access. I downloaded three new Audible books onto my cell phone and my computer. I made sure my trip was highly productive and full of education. There was no way I was going to waste sixteen hours doing nothing. I want to spend as much time as possible acting like a rich person so that is what I become good at.

Driving in a car might become obsolete someday but probably not in my lifetime. Using your car to get places is a fact of life. Unfortunately, when we are driving to the store, work or to visit family and friends, we are using a lot of time. Most people do nothing with this time; they put on the radio, use their cell phones to listen to music and news, talk on the phone or worse, carry on a text conversation. One of the original self-improvement gurus named Jim Rohn had a term for using your driving time to create self-education. He called this self-education during driving time "Automobile University." Mr. Rohn recommended listening to motivational and educational content when you are driving. I almost never listen to news or music on the radio or my cell phone anymore. I use my cell phone to play Audible books and podcasts of motivational, educational and wealth building recordings. I have a whole collection of books on Audible that I play in my car if I am taking longer trips like driving to Pittsburgh to visit my sisters. Driving in your car is the perfect time to work on self-education. Use your driving time to spend more time acting like a rich person.

In our modern era of texting and tweeting our smartphones have the power to be huge time wasters in our lives. It's hard to stop looking down every 5-10 minutes to check notifications, isn't it? It's a good practice to keep your phone off altogether, or at least on vibrate, and let your calls go directly to voicemail.

Then block out 2-3 time slots a day to handle the messages you've received. In this way, you can keep your communication with other people as efficient as possible. Also consider texting people back instead of returning their calls. It takes much less time to send a 3-4 sentence text than it does to have a 15-minute phone conversation.

We're all unique individuals and face different sorts of time wasters. The bottom line is we'll all spend some time in our lives waiting, traveling, or communicating with other people. It's up to each of us to figure out ways to make these activities the most effective.

Life Maintenance

The life maintenance category is an interesting category when it comes to changing what you do with your time. No matter who we are, we all need to take care of certain life maintenance functions. Things like cooking, grocery shopping, paying bills, mowing the lawn, laundry, and cleaning the house all take time away from the higher-level tasks of improving yourself and making money.

It's true that these chores are necessary, but it's also true that many of them can be outsourced. Depending on where you are financially, paying another person to shop for your groceries, clean your house, cut your grass, or do your laundry might be a great thing to consider. Even if it's not an option right now, eventually, as you build your wealth, you might want to hire someone to take care of these life maintenance jobs.

Make sure you are paying your bills online, you are using your bank's cell phone check deposit app, and you get your paycheck direct deposited into your bank account. Do everything you can to avoid driving to the bank and standing in line for a teller or waiting in line at the drive-thru lanes. Also, eliminate the need for driving around by ordering your groceries online and having them delivered so you can save time-consuming trips to the grocery store. Buy household products online and have them delivered.

There is no reason you should have to waste time when you are waiting for something. With cell phones, tablets, notebook PCs, and Wi-Fi available almost everywhere, there is no reason to waste time waiting. The other day I was waiting for the car dealership to put the license plate on my new car lease. They said it would only take ten minutes. I pulled out my cell phone and answered four emails, sent two texts, and made two calls. If you are waiting in line or for an appointment in a reception area, plug in your ear buds and listen to your Audible book, open Kindle on your phone and start reading an eBook, or answer messages and make calls. Prune your contacts, review and delete old text messages, organize your video and audio recordings, or organize and delete photos on your phone. If you're waiting, you might as well be learning or earning.

I do not cut grass, shovel snow or do home repairs. I own income producing rental properties and the professionals and contractors I use to maintain those properties also take care of these tasks at my home. Fortunately for me, my wife likes to go grocery shopping and cook. If she did not like to cook and buy groceries, then we would have a personal assistant doing these tasks for us. My administrative assistant pays the bills for my income producing rental properties and my real estate brokerage.

I have reached the point where I only want to do four things with my time:

1. Self-educate
2. Make money
3. Have fun and relax
4. Help people less fortunate than me

When it comes to life maintenance tasks such as laundry, cooking, cleaning, shoveling snow or cutting grass, these tasks don't pay me, they are not fun, I don't learn anything when I am doing them, and they do not benefit other people.

When a life maintenance task arises, I ask myself if it will help me increase my knowledge, make money, bring enjoyment to me or will it help other people. If not, then I try to hire it out, ask someone else to do it or avoid it.

Socializing and Entertainment

As humans, we can't work all the time. Sometimes we need to simply relax with ourselves or our loved ones. Other times, we go to movies, concerts, or restaurants. We spend time on social media or Gaming. We spend time pursuing our hobbies and personal interests. Although we all need time to enjoy, we can still consider whether we are taking too much time for socializing and entertainment. The key here is to find the work-life balance that works for you.

We all want to spend time with our families and friends, but if all we do is attend social functions, watch Netflix, use social media, and play video games, then we won't have very much time left over to work on improving our own lives.

Excessive entertainment time can eat into the hours we have left for personal improvement and getting rich, as well. The average American spends 2-5 hours per day watching TV, using social media, or surfing the Internet. Gamers spend an average of eight hours a week playing video games. As an experiment, try turning the TV off for one month. Much of the programming isn't very good for your mind, anyway. Put the video games and social media aside for thirty days. A lot of video games contain excessive violence and social media has too much drama. You will be amazed how you will fill the time you free up with more productive activities.

How you use your leisure time varies from person to person. If you want to focus on becoming rich, then you should start watching how you spend this time. Remember, whatever you spend a lot of time doing is what you'll be good at. All of us must spend time doing things that aren't necessarily contributing to becoming rich. However, truly rich people don't waste time if they can avoid it and they consider everything they do in the context of becoming and staying successful.

Avoidable Time Wasters

An avoidable time waster is an activity we have complete control over. We decide when we do these things and how much time we spend on them. Even though we enjoy them, these time wasters are not necessary for our quality of life and do little to contribute to changing your life.

Examples of avoidable time wasters are activities like excessive social conversation with your neighbors or coworkers, driving to a retail store or the bank, fantasy sports leagues, sitting on a barstool drinking just because it is the weekend, watching TV, using the internet and social media for entertainment, sleeping in until noon if you don't have to work that day, and playing video games.

One of the founders of the self-improvement and motivation movement, Earl Nightingale called TV "the income reducer." I would call the activities I mentioned above "the income reducers."

First off, don't hang out at the water cooler, the produce section of the grocery store or your front sidewalk talking for an hour with neighbors or acquaintances. When I am getting out of my car in my driveway and my neighbor is in front of his house cutting his grass, I always say hello, but I keep walking. I have stuff to do if I'm going to become rich. Unless your neighbor is a potential mentor, coach or lender then don't hang out discussing politics and the weather for an hour.

If you want to free up time to become rich, then stop playing fantasy sports. This is an avoidable time waster you can cut from your life immediately; it won't hurt at all or reduce your quality of life one bit. I don't play fantasy real estate investing. I do the real thing. I don't play Monopoly. I play the real game of life! Unless all your fantasy sports league buddies are more successful than you, then you need to cut this time-waster and get serious about becoming rich. If you spend a lot of time playing fantasy sports, then that is what you will be good at. I personally don't know anyone who is getting rich playing fantasy sports.

I realize Gaming has becomes a major international entertainment industry. There are professional Gaming leagues and contests. Unless you think you have a lucrative future playing or designing video games then you should give serious consideration to limiting the amount of time you spend on this activity. It is a serious income reducer.

Before I changed my mindset about becoming successful, I used to go out every Friday and Saturday night just because it was the weekend. Not for any other reason.

I just could not stay home on the weekend. I was so afraid I was going to miss something. When I finally realized all that partying was not getting me anywhere, I sat down and figured out how much time and money I was using going out on the weekends. Between getting ready to go out, being out and recovering from being out late, I was using twenty-five hours a week. I was spending hundreds of dollars every weekend. This motivated me to stay home on the weekends and give up alcohol for a while. To this day it is one of the biggest positive changes for me. The impact was immediate and profound.

The saying, 'the early bird catches the worm,' has been around for a long time because it is true. Make the following two time-schedule adjustments to your life. Go to bed early, around 10 p.m. or earlier, and start getting up early. I am convinced that if you get out of bed early every day and avoid staying up late you will be successful.

Most of the high net worth successful investors I know go to bed early and get up early. If you are setting a big goal for yourself, don't waste your evenings watching TV. Go to bed early and hit the ground running first thing in the morning. Get your workout, breakfast, and morning rituals out of the way and then get started on building your dream life.

Do you know how I found the time to write this book? I did it while I was working 60-70 hours a week starting my real estate brokerage. I decided to go to bed at 9:30 p.m. every night and get out of bed at 6 a.m. every morning. From 6-7 a.m. every morning, I worked on making this book a reality. After work I would do laundry, buy groceries, go to the gym, etc. I felt that the time from 9:30 p.m. or later was wasted time. It was too late to work on the book and the gym was closed. I don't like shopping for groceries at midnight. I used to do that when I was in college. I just shifted my day and used any time after 9:30 p.m. to sleep so I could start my day earlier. This had an enormous impact on my ability to complete this book. The bottom line is you will be successful if you have a longer day rather than a longer night.

There are numerous great reasons to go to bed early and get up early:

- You will be mentally recharged in your most creative state of mind.
- The outside world does not get up early, so you will have minimal interruptions.
- Once your workday gets going, it is too hard to stop and self-educate or build and create your product or service.
- You will start freeing up time to change your life and become rich.
- You will be acting like a rich person.
- Studies show the later you go to bed the unhealthier you will be.

I'm not talking about getting out of bed at 4:30 a.m. every day, but the earlier the better. If you want to change your life and pursue becoming rich, you are either going to do it on the front end of your day or the back end of your day. You are more productive, less tired, and less distracted in the beginning of the day.

Don't want to get up early? Neither did I. I live in a cold, northern climate. Getting out of bed at 6 a.m. wasn't the easiest for me until I discovered a few tricks to make it easier. I bought myself a warm robe and slippers and set a timer with an oil-filled electric space heater that heated my room 30 minutes before it was time to get up. I also used a timer to turn on a soft night light 15-30 minutes before I was due to wake up—this helped my system get used to the idea that it was almost time to get out of bed. Once I was out of bed, I would drink a pint of water, spend 10 minutes writing down some affirmations and practicing gratitude to jump start my day with positive and creative thoughts.

Self-education

This category is the game changer if you want to become rich. If you decide to guard your time and change how you live your life, then self-education is the moneymaker. All rich people incorporate self-education in their life on a regular basis. This is the single biggest change I made to my life that has continually added to my income, wealth, and happiness. You must free up time for this category if you want to change your life and become rich. This category is why you are trying to free up time in the first place. The more time you spend self-educating the better your chances are of changing your life and becoming rich.

Forms of self-education include:
- Reading this book
- Meeting with and communicating with your mentor
- Meeting with your Mastermind group
- Attending seminars and conferences
- Reading non-fiction books about self-improvement and investing
- Watching videos and listening to podcasts
- Listening to Audible downloads or audio recordings

Remember you want to learn from the right people. Look for a great mentor and try to join a Mastermind group. Listen to audio books or podcasts that help you educate and improve yourself while you're waiting for things or driving. You can download the app Audible onto your cell phone—it will allow you to download or stream audiobooks even during those times you don't have Wi-Fi access. I get some of my best self-education done when I'm on a long car ride or a plane or otherwise waiting for something else in my life. If you can't afford to buy books on Audible, most public libraries have free audio books you can download.

Below are ten books I recommend you purchase in eBook, hardcopy, or Audible downloads for your self-education library, if you are serious about becoming rich.

- *The Power of Positive Thinking* by Norman Vincent Peale
- *The One Thing* by Gary Keller
- *The 7 Habits of Highly Effective People* by Stephen Covey
- *The Secret* by Rhonda Byrne
- *Think and Grow Rich* by Napoleon Hill
- *The Strangest Secret* by Earl Nightingale

- *Rich Dad Poor Dad* by Robert Kiyosaki
- *Rich Dad's Cashflow Quadrant* by Robert Kiyosaki
- *The Seven Levels of Communication* by Michael Maher
- *The Richest Man in Babylon* by George S. Clason

I highly recommend you follow these entrepreneurs on their YouTube channels or their podcast feeds:

- Patrick Bet-David
- Eric Thomas
- Earl Nightingale
- Jim Rohn
- Les Brown
- Tony Robbins
- Zig Ziglar
- Pat Flynn
- Tim Ferriss
- Gary Vaynerchuk
- Tai Lopez
- Any TED Talk
- Rod Khleif
- Tom Bilyeu
- Dave Ramsey

Seminars are typically live events in a classroom led by an instructor who is a specialist on a specific topic. The topics usually involve improving some aspect of your life, building wealth, investing or an industry specific skill set. Seminars are usually one to three days and cost anywhere from $195 to $2000. Seminars are great for downloading a large amount of knowledge, experience, and education in a brief time-period, from an expert who has spent years acquiring that information. Would you agree that it is worth spending a few hundred dollars and a few days to acquire success in a discipline instead of spending several years, making numerous mistakes, and spending who knows how much to get to the same place? The value seminars bring to you are well worth the cost of admission and your time. I try to attend at least one seminar a year on success, wealth building or real estate investing. Make it a goal every year to attend at least one seminar to help you achieve success and become rich.

Conventions are large gatherings of professionals from a specific industry. The goal of the convention is to announce all the important advancements in that industry, review how the market for that industry performed over the past year and to forecast where that industry is heading in the upcoming months and years. Most conventions have a trade show floor with vendors that can provide tools, systems and technology for the people and companies that work in that industry. Each day there are breakout sessions with speakers on specific topics. These breakout sessions are like mini-seminars. It is also common for the convention to bring in a nationally known keynote speaker. At the end of the day, they have social and networking events. Conventions usually run two to five days and are held in resort destinations. Almost every industry or market has an annual convention.

I always attend the National Association of Realtors annual convention. Over 20,000 realtors and brokers attended the 2017 annual NAR convention in Chicago. Michael Phelps, the most decorated Olympic swimmer in the history of the sport was the keynote speaker.

Creating Passive Income and Building Wealth

Do you remember the discussion earlier in the book about what it means to be rich? As I stated earlier, you are not rich because you have a lot of money or assets. You acquire income and assets because you think and act like a rich person. Being rich isn't the result of having money. Having money is the result of thinking and acting rich.

Creating passive income and building wealth is what happens when you spend enough time thinking and acting like a rich person. The beliefs, wisdom, knowledge, and mindset offered in this book will lead you to acquire investments and start businesses that will help you create passive income and build wealth. Examples of things you can do to get to this point would be trading stocks, developing your own online affiliate companies, marketing your services or products, buying income-producing rental property, selling products or your own expertise online, starting a multi-level marketing company, or selling advertising on your blog, podcast, or YouTube channel.

A plethora of books and other learning tools exist that talk about all the above passive income-producing ideas. It's beyond the scope of this book to describe each of them here. I personally prefer income-producing rental property as a passive income generator. I am also always expanding my education business by creating books, seminars, home study courses, etc., to help others achieve success, happiness, and wealth.

If you focus on spending as much time as possible implementing the knowledge, beliefs and concepts from this book, you will eventually own the assets listed above. Whatever you spend a lot of time doing, that is what you will be good at. Spend a lot time acting rich, and before you know it, you will own assets like the ones above.

Tracking your time

It is amazing how little we know about our own habits and actions. We just don't realize how much money, time, or effort we spend on things until we make a conscious effort to track and record the real facts. If your goal is to stop wasting time so you can spend more hours acting like a rich person, then you need to know where all your time is going. Do you really know how much time you are spending on your daily activities? You might think you do, but trust me, you have no idea how much time you are wasting until you start writing it down.

A good example of this is when I was working out a lot at the gym, and I was frustrated that I could not gain any weight. One day, I was describing this weight gain problem to a guy who was a power lifter. He told me I wasn't eating enough. I said that could not be the problem because I was eating all the time. He told me to get a notebook and for thirty days write down everything I put in my mouth and how many calories each item I ate contained.

When I started tracking my food intake, I weighed 140 pounds. According to the Basal Metabolic Rate and the Harris Benedict equation, I needed 1800 calories per day to maintain that weight. I was sure I was getting more than 1800 calories. Within a couple weeks of recording everything I ate, I determined I was only taking in 1880 calories. I could not believe it. I would have never believed it without writing it down in that book and tracking what I was really eating.

Based on the results of that tracking, I created a meal plan to consume 2500 calories a day and within three months I gained thirty pounds, weighing in at 170 pounds. My strength and size in the gym shot right up.

Another great example of the value of tracking time and results is the MS Excel file I use to track all my closed real estate transactions. From the very first year I became a real estate agent, I decided to record several pieces of information whenever I closed a real estate deal. I used a simple MS Excel file to track eight columns of data about every closed deal. One of the most important columns was the type of deal I closed. Was it Residential, Investment, Commercial, Business or Land? After a couple of years of tracking data, it become clear to me that 95% of my closed deals were Residential, Investment and Commercial. As I moved forward in my career, I focused on those categories of real estate, and I avoided Business and Land deals because even though I spent time on those deals I didn't close very many of them. This focus allowed me to dedicate all my time to transactions that had a higher likelihood of closing. Also, tracking this data made me realize my number one source of clients were people I already knew, repeat business and referral business from past clients. With this information in hand, I focused on my past client relationship program to generate even more repeat and referral business. The payback was more closed deals and higher income. I would have never known this if I wasn't tracking my closed deals.

The point of these stories is to show you the value of tracking what you are doing so you can make the necessary changes to reach your goal. If you don't really know what you are doing, then how can you make the adjustments that lead to success?

Purchase a small journal and start tracking the time you spend doing things. Do this for 60 days, using the time categories outlined in this chapter, and see where your time is going. If you are like most people, you will need to stop wasting time if you want to spend more time acting like a rich person. You can't free up time if you don't know where your time is going in the first place.

Below is an example of how you could analyze where you're currently using your time.

Based on a 24-hour day and 365 days in a year, we all get 8,760 hours a year to live our lives:
24 hours X 365 days = **8,760 hours**

If you sleep seven hours a night, then you will be sleeping **2,555 hours** per year.

If you eat three meals per day and it takes 30 minutes to eat each meal, then you spend 1.5 hours per day X 365 days = **548 hours** per year eating.

Let's allow two hours per day for hygiene and three hours a week for exercise. Let's add 10 hours a year for doctors and dentists. The total time used annually for hygiene and health is:
(Two hours X 365 days) + (Three hours x 52 weeks) + Ten hours per year = **896 hours** per year.

If you work 40 hours a week and you receive two weeks of vacation time a year from your employer, then you are working 50 weeks out of the year. You will be working at your current source of income **2,000 hours** a year.

Let's estimate that unexpected interruptions, emergencies, and accidents use three hours a month, so that is **36 hours** per year.

Let's estimate 1 hour per day for unavoidable time

wasters which covers all the time you spend waiting, traveling, or communicating. One-hour x 365 Days = **365 hours** per year.

The total time estimated for the Life Maintenance category is Eight hours per week or **416 hours** per year.

Next, let's estimate some time for socializing and entertainment. If you take two vacation weeks a year that is 14 days x 24 hours = **366 hours** per year.

If you are married and you have children, let's estimate you spend at least three hours a day giving your family love, support, and affection. If you are involved with your kid's sports activities, then this number is probably higher. It is hard for me to attach an accurate time usage to this task because I don't know your family status. The three hours also covers socializing with friends, neighbors, coworkers, and relatives.
Three hours x 365 days = **1095 hours** per year.

The average American spends two to five hours per day watching TV, using social media, or Internet-based entertainment each day. Let's be optimistic and only use one hour per day for this:
One-hour x 365 days = **365 hours** per year.

I don't know if you like movies at the theatre or if you can afford to eat out at restaurants. I'm sure you have a hobby or personal interest. Let's estimate we all spend an average of 2 hours a week on these time usages:
Two hours per week x 52 weeks = **104 hours** per year.

Below is our grand total estimate time used annually to live our lives:
$2555+548+896+2000+36+365+416+366+1095+365+104$ = **8746 hours** per year.

This estimate of how you live your life is only 14 hours per year less than the 8,760 hours you have available each year. I did not try to make these numbers close. I just estimated the time usage in each category by doing some research online and using my own personal experiences.

Unfortunately, this does leave much time to change your life through self-education, creating passive income, or wealth building.

Time is an incredible Life Asset! I hope this chapter gives you some ideas about how to make the best use of your time. It's crucial for you to carve out hours for self-education and self-improvement, which are the only paths to wealth and happiness. If you want to change your life and become rich, then you must stop wasting time. Rich people don't waste time if they can avoid it and they hire people to do things for them when they can. Remember, whatever you spend a lot of time doing, that is what you will be good at.

ASSET #4: KNOWLEDGE

BECOME A LIFELONG LEARNER

*"Education is the most powerful weapon
which you can use to change the world."*
—Nelson Mandela

Love is one of the most powerful emotions in the world. It can make a person obsessive at times, it can make you take massive action, and it can remove you from your comfort zone. As for me, I love *Self-education.* I obsess about it. After learning things, I take massive action. And, yes, my self-education does indeed remove me from my comfort zone.

I just can't get enough knowledge. After I finish a 12-hour day at my company, I go home and watch YouTube videos about wealth building, marketing, social media techniques, investing, personal improvement, and health. I love seeking knowledge and becoming a better person through that knowledge. I'm in love with constantly evolving and improving. Once when I was out to dinner with my wife and some other couples, I snuck off to the restroom three times to listen to some audio recordings on personal improvement because I was so into what I was hearing. I couldn't put it down. My wife asked me if I was sick because I kept going to the restroom!

This love of learning, self-education and pursuit of knowledge is another difference that separates rich people from those with a poverty mindset. Rich people understand the direct connection between their success and their self-education. The richest people in the world are the most successful learners. Rich people are always pursuing more knowledge. People who haven't found success often think education is merely a necessary and temporary hoop to jump through just to get a job.

Rich people know the more they learn, the more they earn. They are lifelong learners because they realize their self-education and knowledge is the way to increase their income and net worth. The wealthiest people in the world block out time on a regular basis to read books, attend seminars and conferences, and pay mentors and coaches to help them learn the skills necessary to grow their wealth. Warren Buffett reads two hours every day. Bill Gates takes a two-week vacation every year to focus on reading books. Many people haven't read a non-fiction book in years and typically use social media and television for entertainment purposes only.

When I took my fly-fishing trip to Kiritimati Island last year, I couldn't wait for the plane to take off. I was so excited that I would be spending the next nine hours working on this book and listening to audiobooks about how to start an online education business. A couple of years ago I took a vacation to Punta Cana with my wife. I read *Think and Grow Rich* on the flight down and finished it by the pool that week. Now, that's my idea of a vacation!

Many people view education as a dreaded task or process that they can't wait to complete. Unfortunately, many assume they only need to graduate from high school or college to get a job and many others haven't even had much education beyond high school. The problem lies in the fact that typical jobs for those with only a high school diploma don't pay very well. It is getting harder and harder to find a job after graduation from college. These jobs only allow you to trade your time for money, which has limited income potential.

Rich people view education as an investment for their future, not a necessary task. I truly believe the best investment you can ever make is educating yourself. Your mind is the most important asset you own. If you want to become a better person and become financially successful, then you must invest in yourself every chance you get.

If you want to change your life and become rich, you need to be obsessed with changing the way you think, act, and believe by making self-education a passion and a priority. You must fall in love with lifelong education.

Self-education is a lifelong pursuit

Self-education is not a one-time task. It is part of the lifestyle of being rich. If you make it a one-time task, then the benefit is a one-time benefit. Self-education is like the sun and water to a plant. If you water the plant often and give it sunlight, it will keep growing and producing flowers or fruit. Your income and net worth are like the plant, and knowledge is the water and sun for that plant. Keep providing your life with education and knowledge and your income will keep growing and your net worth will increase.

If you want to change your life and become rich, then you must change your view on education. Stop viewing education as a burden or a task. Rich people view education as a fun investment they are passionate about. Rich people can't wait to start reading the next book or listening to the next podcast or webinar. I always have my next book on my desk waiting to be read before I am finished with the book I am currently reading. I am always stoked whenever I have another seminar or conference in my schedule. I have become a self-education junkie because I have learned how my self-education is the fuel that is growing my life in incredible ways. The more I learn, the more I earn. I believe a lifelong attitude of learning is mandatory if you want to become rich.

Education is a rich person's best friend. How do you treat your best friend? You interact with your best friend all the time. You can't wait to see them. You plan to spend time with them. Self-improvement author John Maxwell's perspective is that if he focuses on personal improvement and education, he can't help but accomplish all his goals. His goals keep coming automatically because he is always growing as a person and a professional.

Your income is directly proportional to the value you bring to other people. You can increase the value you bring to other people if you increase your knowledge, wisdom, and skill sets. This can only be done with self-education and the lifestyle of lifelong learning.

If I told you I have a great seminar on getting rich, you would jump on the opportunity. But if I told you I have a great seminar on personal improvement, you might not be as interested. Many people don't understand that, as you improve yourself, your life will change for the better and lead to wealth and success. Being rich is a mindset and a lifestyle. Change your mindset to that of a rich person, and the money will follow. Your financial situation reflects where you are on the personal improvement ladder. If you want more money, then work on improving you.

If your life is not where you want it, and it has not grown or changed for a long time, it is because you have not changed as a person. Your inability to change is caused by your lack of continued education. You are lacking personal development. If you don't pursue personal development throughout your life, then your emotional, social, professional, and financial growth will stop.

Increasing your knowledge through continued personal development is a superpower! It can change your communication skills, how you handle your money, and how healthy you are. Through self-education, you can also change the way you think, how you socialize, the language you use, what you do with your time and money, the decisions you make, and your confidence level.

You don't listen to one podcast episode or one YouTube video and become rich. You become and remain rich by making self-education and personal improvement a regular part of your life. You don't go to the gym once and walk out with a great body. It takes work, dedication, and a long-term commitment to maintain your healthy figure. Becoming rich and staying rich requires continued self-education and personal improvement. Learning must be a lifelong passion if you want to maintain your wealth.

Self-education has a wonderful motivational effect on you. In my opinion, Zig Ziglar was right on the money when he said: "People often say motivation doesn't last. Neither does bathing—that's why we recommend it daily." Sometimes at night I watch YouTube videos of motivational speakers just to inspire me for the next day. As soon as my eyes open the next morning, I want to jump out of bed, already motivated to succeed.

Formal education versus self-education

"Your formal education will get you a job,
but your self-education will make you a fortune."
--Zig Ziglar

Your formal education will help you learn a specific skill set so you can get a job. The purpose of a formal school education is to prepare you for jobs as a factory worker, restaurant employee, secretary, nurse, beautician, engineer, etc. Examples of your formal education are grade school, middle school, high school, technical or vocational school, and college. These education sources give you a degree or a certificate that you can use to prove you finished the educational program and help you qualify for a job. They have a start date and an end date. They typically have days and times when you must be in attendance, although many formal education sources are moving online. Most people can't wait to complete these experiences and only pursue these sources because it is necessary to get a job.

Your self-education, on the other hand, can come from many sources and typically revolves around personal, health, or financial improvement. You never finish your self-education like you do a formal education program. You don't get a degree or certificate that helps you apply for jobs. Self-education is not mandatory and is only pursued if someone is passionate about changing their life and growing as a person. There are no set times or dates for this education.

Today we have more knowledge at our fingertips than ever before. The time to succeed is now and it is easier than ever. The Internet and the explosion of online learning resources are making it easier, less expensive, and more convenient to change your life for the better. We live in a time with more abundance and opportunity than ever in the history of the world. In the past, you had to learn from your parents or your formal education. Today, millions of people are online sharing their knowledge, beliefs, and skills.

Leveraging other people's knowledge is one of the fastest and most efficient ways to change your life and learn quickly. Remember this statement: "It is okay to learn from mistakes, just make sure they are someone else's."

Udacity, Udemy, Skillshare and YouTube are the most popular online platforms today for both free and paid life-changing education. You can download the RSS (Really Simple Syndication) feed to your cell phone for limitless podcasts from successful mentors sharing their stories. In the last chapter, I mentioned some of the mentors I follow on YouTube, podcasts, and audiobooks. People like Gary Vaynerchuk, Tai Lopez, Pat Flynn, Brandon Bouchard, Tom Bilyeu, Zig Ziglar, and Jim Rohn have really helped me with their knowledge.

Popular self-education and personal improvement

topics cover just about everything. You can learn how to:

- Develop a positive attitude.
- Sleep better at night.
- Remove stress from your life.
- Embrace a better diet.
- Start your own business.
- Invest in real estate or stocks.
- Get out of debt.
- Find people to loan you money.
- Maximize your social media skills.
- Market your business.
- Negotiate and communicate.
- Set goals and plan.
- Begin a multi-level marketing business.
- Start your own YouTube channel.
- Start your own podcast.

The School of Wealth

It always fascinates me how some folks think rich people are snobs or elitists because they only associate with other rich people. Most rich people are not snobs. And they don't dislike people who have less money, less education, or less success than them. There are a lot of very generous and kind rich people out there. Rich and successful people spend their time with other rich and successful people because they learn from each other.

The School of Wealth is a phrase I coined to refer to an invisible club or society that rich people have access to that others do not. Where is this School of Wealth located, you might ask? Where do you get this financial and success education? I say it is invisible because there is no brick and mortar building called 'The School of Wealth.' I have never met a person with a degree from this 'School.'

This is how The School of Wealth works. Most people have never been taught how to properly earn enough money, keep it, and use it effectively during their lifetime. You see, formal education may affect how much earned income you make in a salaried or hourly paying job, but it has nothing to do with *real* financial independence.

Most people spend 13-20 years going to school to learn how to earn money at a job, but they spend little or no time teaching themselves how to keep and grow what they earned. They don't learn how to make their money work for them. After they get a job, they stop educating themselves completely. They don't learn how to think like rich people and let their money work for them.

Those who have acquired wealth are all well educated in the art of making, growing, and retaining money. This education was not acquired through a conventional school or university; it was acquired at... you guessed it. The School of Wealth.

Our public schools were structured to create workers, not investors. The School of Wealth is how wealthy people learn what wealth is and how to acquire it. People 'attending' this School surround themselves with others who are already wealthy. This includes their parents, relatives, friends, coworkers, and bosses. They also learn from other successful people they meet at seminars and conferences. If you are like most people, you might not have had the opportunity to be exposed to those who understood the principles of wealth and success. If your parents, siblings and relatives are not people with an abundance and wealth mindset then chances are you grew up with their poverty mindset. In the past people who grow up with the poverty mindset had little chance to change it because of a lack of access to the people with an abundance and wealth mindset. They did not have access to the School of Wealth.

I have some fantastic news for you. With the beliefs, knowledge, and principles in this book and others like it, as well as the amazing opportunities that the Internet has created, the doors to The School of Wealth are now wide open to you. And, best of all, the tuition is free! In our world of technology, you have access to many amazing people who are waiting to help you change your life for the better. You now have the same opportunity and education available to you as everyone else.

Make time for personal improvement and self-education

The wonderful thing about self-education and lifelong learning is that you can fit it into your schedule. Be careful, though, not to keep putting off this critical part of changing your life. It is way too easy to keep saying, "Oh, I'll start tomorrow." Don't be afraid to block out time for self-education. Live your life around your self-education, not the other way around.

Using some good planning techniques will help you leverage your time for self-education and personal improvement. I always have a couple of audiobooks on my phone that I'm listening to. No matter what the situation, if I get a few minutes I pop in my ear buds and start listening to books about money, health, or business. It is truly liberating and motivating to feel your confidence and self-esteem grow from self-education.

If you truly fall in love with personal improvement and self-education, you will start to make it a priority. You will want to do it more than anything else. You'll start using your time to self-educate. And you'll do it because you'll see the rewards immediately in your life.

The Education Quiz

Another great clip from one of Jim Rohn's audio recordings is from a time when Jim was not yet the great personal improvement guru he has become. At the time of the clip, Jim was not doing well in life. He was broke. His life had not changed or improved in over five years. He had just met his first mentor, who asked him the following questions: *How many books have you read in the past month? How many seminars have you attended in the past three months? How much money have you saved in the past year?*

Jim's answer to all these questions was "None."

This story illustrates the fact that, because Jim had not changed his life, his income and savings had not changed either. His mentor was telling him that he needed to change if he wanted his money or job status to improve. Self-education is the number one way you can change. Changing yourself is what becoming rich is all about.

Ask yourself the following questions:

- How many non-fiction books have you read in the past year?
- How may seminars or conferences have you attended in the past year?
- When was the last time your formal educational level increased?
- How many YouTube videos about investing,

business, or entrepreneurship have you watched in the past month?

- Whose podcasts are you currently listening to?
- Do you have any written goals?
- How much has your income increased over the past five years?
- How much money do you have in savings?
- How much money do you have in retirement accounts?
- If you lose your job tomorrow, can you still pay your bills?
- Is your credit score above 700?

Ten must-do self-education habits and goals

Below is a list of changes you can make now that cost very little money but will have an instant and significant impact on your self-education, personal improvement, and knowledge:

1. Make sure you read this book completely and follow its advice and habits.
2. Stop watching TV or using social media for entertainment.
3. Minimize the time you spend on socializing and entertainment.
4. Stop watching sports every weekend.
5. Stop going out to bars and clubs unless it is a special occasion.
6. Download the Audible app to your cell phone.
7. Start following the YouTube and podcast channels from the list of self-improvement gurus I've mentioned earlier in this book.

8. Read books that teach you how to improve your life.
9. Attend a live seminar that teaches something you are passionate about.
10. Join a club or group of people who are enthusiastic about the same goals you have.

The richest people in the world are the best learners in the world. If you want to change your life and become rich, you must become a great learner. Learners are earners. You can only increase the value you bring to other people by becoming a learner and embracing the lifelong pursuit of self-education and knowledge.

ASSET #5: MONEY

CONTROL YOUR FINANCES

"Money isn't everything, but it's right up there with oxygen."
—Zig Ziglar

What does the American dream mean for you? For me it means I can quit my job to do what I want, when and where I want. It means I will have passive income from my assets and investments that will support my ideal standard of living and allow me to continue to grow my income and net worth.

My ideal American dream includes having the time and money to help other people, owning my home free and clear of debt, being able to take vacations when I want, having multiple sources of passive income, and have adequate health and life insurance. I can maintain my standard of living even if I quit my job—or, if my life partner or I get sick, we can still pay our bills. The American dream means I have great credit, I am debt free, and I have cash in the bank.

Although popular media would like you to believe that the American dream is dead, I don't believe it is. It is true that the old way of working the same job for 30 years and retiring with a pension has gone away. This financial model has been replaced with an entirely new set of opportunities and abundance. A new American dream.

The American dream is a lifestyle that is realistic for anyone, if you only know how to look for it. If you are willing to work smart and hard over time, bringing value to other people, you can have an extraordinary life of financial freedom. To do this, you need to take control of your finances. Now is the time to prepare for this new American dream.

The Financial Fitness Quiz

Due to constant advances in medical technology, studies show we are going to live longer. That means we will need more money to support our increasing longevity. If you combine that with the future of the employee being in jeopardy due to automation, robotics, and artificial intelligence, you need to get serious about your money, your financial literacy, and how you will make a living in the future.

On social media people take all kinds of quizzes. You can find out what kind of dog you'd be or who your perfect soulmate is. That's all well and good, but why not take a quiz that will help you improve your life? Below is my 'Financial Fitness' quiz.

If you want to know how financially fit you are, then answer the following questions as honestly as you can. These questions will assess your current and future financial status.

1. Has your annual income increased at least 3.5% a year over the past five years?
2. Are you saving at least 10% of your take-home pay every month?
3. If you lose your job tomorrow, can you still pay all your bills?
4. If your furnace breaks down tomorrow, can you pay an estimated $2,500 for a new one without using a credit card or another form of debt or asking a family member for a loan?
5. If you or your partner pass away tomorrow, can your family continue to pay all the bills and provide a proper burial?
6. If you or your partner pass away tomorrow, do you have enough life insurance to replace their income?
7. Have you updated your Personal Financial Statement within the past twelve months?
8. If the industry in which you are currently employed becomes obsolete tomorrow, do you have a backup plan to pursue the same amount of income doing something else?
9. Do you have a liquid cash emergency fund equal to six months of your take-home pay?
10. When you reach age 67, will your retirement plan pay you at least 75% of your current annual income until you reach the age of ninety?
11. Is your credit score 700 or higher?
12. Do you have a Last Will and Testament, Power of Attorney, Living Will and Health Care Power of Attorney?

If you answered NO to more than half of these questions, then you need to get serious about your financial future.

The six critical steps to a better financial future

If you did not do well with the Financial Fitness quiz above, don't worry too much. Most people don't do well. The good news is that it is very realistic for all of us to turn our financial situation around and create a healthy financial future. It is very simple to outline the changes that need to be made. I will be honest with you though—it isn't always easy to change your finances. Change of any kind isn't easy. Almost anything worth having in life requires effort and change.

I look at it this way: if you are broke and struggling financially, you are probably suffering. So, if you're suffering anyway, why not suffer to make your life better? Why not suffer and sacrifice to have the life you desire? I have made those sacrifices and put in the work and now I am realizing the new American dream every day. Life is good for me and it can be for you, too, if you want it. It is doable for everyone.

Below is a list of changes every person should make if they want to pursue financial freedom and acquire the American dream. This book would double in size if we got into a discussion about the numerous types of assets and passive income that exist today. The Internet is full of books, audio recordings, YouTube videos, podcasts, and online courses about how to pursue passive income, investing, and wealth building. For now, I want to cover the most important basics for turning your financial future around. These include:

1. Get lean and mean.
2. Start practicing delayed gratification.

3. Maximize your current income.
4. Get out of debt.
5. Fix your credit.
6. Get educated about how money works.
7. Save 5-10% of everything you earn.

Get lean and mean

Cutting unnecessary spending, getting out of debt, and saving money alone will not make you rich. As I have mentioned numerous times in this book, becoming rich is about changing the way you think, what you believe, how you make decisions, and who you surround yourself with. But once you understand and begin to act, think, and believe like a rich person, you are going to need money to start investing in yourself and in cash flow-producing assets. Taking control of your money is critical if you want to invest in yourself, a business idea, real estate, or stocks and mutual funds.

Not everyone has a bunch of money left over at the end of the month that they don't know what to do with. People with a poverty mindset find themselves without a lot of money because of their lack of education, negative belief systems, and bad decision-making skills. These things lead to a lack of money.

Rich people, on the other hand, are rich because they guard their money. They only spend money on things that bring value to their life. They spend money on the essentials like having a comfortable home to live in, transportation, food, and healthcare. They also spend money on education and investments. I'm not saying rich people don't splurge and buy nice homes, luxury cars, or vacations, but they only do that after they have the comfortable cushion of wealth. This book is about how to become rich. It is not about how to live rich.

If you want to change your life and become rich, then stop spending money on anything unless you absolutely need it. You must pay your mortgage or your rent or you won't have a roof over your head. You must make your car payments and put gas in your car, or you won't be able to get to work. You need food. You must pay your electric and gas bills, so you can have lights and heat in your home. I understand that you must pay your bills. These expenses are unavoidable.

When I talk about giving things up, I'm talking about relinquishing things you can live without. The operative phrase here is "things you can live without." You can't live without food, but you can live without alcohol. You can't live without a roof over your head, but you can live without gambling. You can't live without heat and lights in your home, but you can live without cable TV. You can't live without food, but you can stop eating out at expensive restaurants and buying expensive coffee. Another benefit of cooking lunch and dinner at home is you will probably eat heathier.

There is a never-ending list of things we all spend money on that can be put off for a while—or even eliminated altogether. If you are serious about changing your life and becoming rich, then you will need to delay spending money on things you can live without.

If you want to change your life and become rich, then you need to embrace the concept of delayed gratification. I am only proposing living lean and mean until you get to a place in life where you can afford to take all the vacations and drink all the Starbucks coffee you want. Below is the definition of 'Delayed Gratification' from Wikipedia.

"Delayed gratification, or deferred gratification, describes the process that the subject undergoes when the subject resists the temptation of an immediate reward in preference for a later reward. Generally, delayed gratification is associated with resisting a smaller but more immediate reward to receive a larger or more enduring reward later. A growing body of literature has linked the ability to delay gratification to a host of other positive outcomes, including academic success, physical health, psychological health, social competence and financial freedom."

Many of us have a problem waiting for things and sacrificing our immediate gratification in the short term in order to enjoy long-term rewards. I mentioned before that taking control of your life and making sacrifices has a positive effect on us. Our confidence and self-esteem grow when we gain that sense of control. Accepting and practicing delayed gratification is critical to support the change needed to become rich. Waiting for things is good for you both mentally and emotionally.

We all make purchases we could live without. Stop eating at restaurants and coffee shops. Start buying groceries, cooking at home, and bagging your lunch. You will save money and eat healthier, too. Give up restaurants like Starbucks and Panera Bread. While these are great places, they also sell overpriced products. Five-dollar coffees at Starbucks are no better than a $1 coffee at the convenience store.

Try not to buy any new clothing unless you absolutely need it. Keep wearing your clothes until they're worn out or no longer fit. If your car is paid off and runs fine, then keep it until it won't get you to where you need to go. Don't buy a car just because the one you have isn't flashy and new anymore. If you must buy a car, then buy a used one. New cars are a huge waste of money and depreciate the moment you drive them off the lot.

Try to resist buying toys and clothes for your pets. Pets need food, water, and love. I don't know about your dogs, but mine just destroy any toys we give them within a couple days anyway. It is like throwing money in the garbage can.

Let's talk about cell phones, cable TV, Netflix, and Sirius radio subscriptions. These technology services cost you a ton of money every month. It might be worth considering reducing your cell phone plan. Unless you use your phone for work, maybe you can reduce your plan to save money. You might not need a huge data plan for your phone unless you use it for work. If you find yourself using a lot of data on your phone merely for entertainment purposes, then shut it off.

Personally, I'm not a big fan of most TV programming. Many of the newer shows startle me with their negativity and violence. I'm sure there are good shows out there, but I prefer to just watch YouTube videos that help me improve my life and educate me. You are the only person who can ultimately decide how important this stuff is to you. But if you're spending a lot of money on technology only for entertainment purposes, it might be worth considering paring down your bills by getting rid of cable or Netflix, at least for a short time. Not only will you save money, but this is a great way to free up time to add self-education to your life.

I don't know how you feel about sharing your living space with another person but renting your extra rooms to a roommate is a fantastic way to get some extra needed cash flow to pay down debt or invest in yourself. If you have an apartment, consider getting a roommate. If you own a home, consider renting your spare bedrooms through a company like Airbnb.

Let's talk about transportation. If you and your life partner each own a car, you could consider going down to one car. Before you call me crazy, give it some consideration. Many of us drive our car to work, where it sits for 8-10 hours in our employer's parking lot. If you or your partner have employment scenarios that do not require a car to perform your work, then it is very realistic to live with one car. Let's say your car payment is around $400, with about $300 spent monthly for car insurance, repairs, and fuel. That's $700 a month. What if you could share a car with your partner or even another person? For 12 months, the savings would be $8,400. What a fantastic way to free up money to pay off a credit card, start an emergency fund, or start a new business! Twelve months is not that long a time period and you can reap so many benefits.

We all spend money on personal grooming products and services to help us look beautiful. The prices companies charge women for beauty products that promise to reverse the aging process are ridiculous. I think these products are a rip-off. Consider whether you really need to pay $20-30 for a bottle of shampoo, or would a $10 product work just as well? Once at a party, I guy I met told me he cuts his own hair. He was the best-looking guy at the party and his hair looked great. Stop paying salons to trim and paint your nails. Do it yourself for a while so you can save money and pay down your bills. It's great to splurge occasionally on these things, but it is better to practice delayed gratification and wait until you get out of debt.

In my opinion, extended families today spend way too much money at Christmas time. Ask your parents, friends, and siblings to skip buying retail gifts for each other for one year so you all can save some money. Come up with another idea to help reduce the money you spend at this expensive time of year. You could each exchange some used personal items as gifts. How about giving each other homemade food or baked goods? Maybe you can agree to all make something from scratch for each other. Do something other than going to all the big-box stores and running up your credit cards.

Alcohol, recreational drugs, and gambling—not only is this stuff a waste of your money, it is not good for your health or your family's future. You will also be surrounding yourself with other people who need these vices—probably not good company for you, anyway. If you won't or can't remove these vices from your life, it will be very hard to become rich. Abusing drugs and alcohol will keep you poor. If you have an addiction, do everything you can to find the help you need to turn your life around. It will be very hard to leave poverty behind if you have addiction problems.

I know giving up cigarettes is one of the hardest vices to quit. Nicotine is a very addictive substance. It is harder to get off nicotine than heroin or cocaine. If there is any way you can quit cigarettes and tobacco products, it will be well worth your effort. We all know how bad cigarettes are for your physical health, but also consider how damaging they are to your financial health. Below is an analysis of what you are giving up financially to be a lifelong smoker.

If you pay an average of $10 for a pack for cigarettes over the next 40 years and you smoke four packs a week, then you'll spend about $2,080 per year. If you invested that $2,080 each year into a mutual fund that paid just a 5% annual return on your money, after 40 years you would have a mutual fund worth $251,264! Do you know how many rental properties you could buy, businesses you could start, or investments you could make with that money?

Maximize your current income

There are only two ways to take control of your finances. You can reduce the amount of money you spend, and you can increase the amount of money you bring in. For the short term, let's make sure you are maximizing your income for your current level of education and expertise. Right now, our goal is to make sure you are getting all the income possible from your current employment or investments. Once you get control of your financial life, you can start to prepare for making investments in your career, real estate, or a business idea.

Ask yourself the following five questions:

1. When was the last time your employer gave you a raise?
2. When was the last time you asked your employer for a raise?
3. When was the last time you received a promotion?
4. When was the last time you asked for a promotion?
5. When was the last time you updated your resume and tried to find a higher paying job?

According to a Career Builder survey, 56% of workers fail to negotiate a better salary. More than half of workers indicated they feel uncomfortable asking for more money. I am a firm believer in the age-old phrase: *ask and you shall receive.* If you don't ask for more money or a promotion, then you probably won't get it. Start asking your employer for more responsibility and more money. Tim Ferriss, one of the counter-cultural thinkers I follow online, has said, "Your success in life depends on the number of uncomfortable conversations you're willing to have."

If your employer does not consider your request, then maybe it's time to move on and up. Get your resume updated and start applying for better paying jobs. If you receive a better job offer, you can always go back to your current employer and give them the opportunity to match the higher pay. If they don't match it, then maybe it is time to move on to a new opportunity.

Get out of debt

This section is a high-level summary of how to get out of debt. Reading books by Suze Orman and Dave Ramsey will give you the micro-details for a complete study of this goal. For now, I want to impress upon you the importance of getting out of debt and how it relates to becoming rich. Dave Ramsey said it best that your earned income is your best wealth building tool. This wealth building tool will not be available to you if you are living paycheck to paycheck because of all your debt.

Trying to become rich is like running in a race. Too much debt is like a ball and chain tied to your ankle. Can you imagine how hard it is to run in a race when you have a ball and chain around your ankle? You won't get too far in that race.

This book is not about how to invest money in assets like real estate, stocks, mutual funds, or your own business. I can tell you from experience that if you are in debt and have poor credit, it will be difficult to make those investments. You need good credit and access to some of your earned income if you want to start acquiring cash flow producing assets or start a business. I have read many books and heard numerous so-called gurus talk about becoming financially free and rich even if you have no money, credit, time, or experience. If this were true, then everyone would be rich. In my world it takes time, hard work, self-education, good credit, and access to money.

Below is a simple plan that has been used by millions of people to eliminate bad debt.

Step one: Stop using any form of credit immediately. This should be something you do for good. Credit cards are not money. Credit cards are financial poison. If you don't have the money, then don't buy the item. It's that simple. If you must use a credit card to buy something, then you can't afford it.

Step two: Make a list of the balances you owe for all your debts and the monthly payment for each debt. Don't include things like heating and electric bills or groceries, which are recurring expenses you can't live without. These expenses are not debt. Instead, forms of debt include car payments, credit cards, store charge accounts, student loans, family loans, outstanding medical bills, home mortgage payments, and home equity lines of credit. When you make your list of the balances you owe, include the name of the creditor, the interest rate, your balance owed, minimum monthly payment due, and any extra payment amount you can commit to making.

It is important to make this list in writing. If you want to accomplish a goal, it must be clearly defined and written down. Also, by writing down your plan and goal, you'll start to make it more obtainable. Below is an example of a debt tracker I made in MS Excel. If you go to your cell phone app store, there are numerous budgeting and debt reducing applications you can download for free.

NAME	TYPE	BALANCE	RATE	MINIMUM PAYMENT	EXTRA PAYMENT
Jones department store	Store Card	$456.76	21.000%	$15.60	$100.00
Discover	Credit Card	$2,345.67	20.000%	$56.79	
PA Loan System	Student Loan	$4,350.00	2.500%	$175.00	
Mazda Financial	Car Loan	$4,567.89	3.500%	$355.00	
Master Card	Credit Card	$6,578.21	14.000%	$87.89	
Student loans of America	Student Loan	$8,907.00	3.500%	$250.00	
Bank of Someplace	Home Equity Loan	$13,450.00	3.500%	$132.42	
Bank of Someplace	Home Mortgage	$73,459.09	4.875%	$879.64	

NOTE: Home Mortgage balance only includes principal balance of the loan.
It does not include interest or escrows for real estae taxes and home insurance.

Step three: Call all your creditors and try to get the interest rates lowered. Tell them if they won't lower the rates, then you are going to pay off the entire balance and close the account. Most creditors don't want you to pay off the debt because that is how they make money from you, by charging you a lot of interest.

Step four: Try to get a consolidation loan with a lower interest rate to pay off several of your debts that have higher interest rates. If you have some equity in your home, a Home Equity Line of Credit (HELOC) is a great way to consolidate debts. The interest rates are typically lower than the rates you are paying on credit cards, store charges, and car loans and you can write off the interest portion of your payment on your tax return.

Step five: Make sure you are always paying at least the minimum payment on time for each debt to avoid surcharges and penalties. Late payments will also keep you from improving your credit score.

Step six: Use all extra available cash you can afford to pay down the loan with the smallest balance. After this loan has been paid off, then move all extra available money to the loan with the next smallest balance. Keep doing this until you eliminate all bad debt.

Getting out of debt is a critical step toward becoming rich. Rich people use debt only to make more money—they don't use debt to buy things. When I am talking about getting out of debt, I am talking about eliminating the bad debt from your life, like credit cards. Getting out of debt will improve your credit score which will help you get loans to buy investments or start a business. Another benefit of getting out of debt is reduced stress and better health. If you want to change your life and become rich, it requires money to invest, start a business, and pay for certain forms of education.

Fix your credit

Improving your credit score is critical when you are ready to start acquiring cash flow producing assets or starting a business. There will be times when you will borrow money to make these acquisitions and your credit score is an important factor in obtaining this financing. You will also receive lower interest rates and lower insurance premiums.

Step one: Go online and get a free copy of your credit history and score. It is important to know where you stand before you start your journey towards financial freedom. The Fair Credit Reporting Act allows you to obtain free copies of your credit reports from the three credit bureaus: Experian, Equifax, and TransUnion, once a year. You can access these free reports from AnnualCreditReport.com. You can also get your reports directly from Experian, Equifax, and TransUnion. It is important to see your report from each of the three credit bureaus because your credit report can differ with each one.

Step two: Fix or remove any errors in the three reports. Do this even if you haven't done the work to raise your credit score. You can go to the websites of each of the three credit bureaus to find the instructions on how to fix any errors. You can also hire a credit repair service to determine if anything on your credit report can be removed or adjusted to help your credit score.

Every time you pay off a debt, make sure it is reflected on each of the credit bureaus reports.

Get educated about how money works

In the chapter about education I talked about becoming a lifelong learner. You can only become rich if you increase the value you bring to other people. You can only do this through a lifelong pursuit of self-education. You need to constantly teach yourself about money: how to earn it, save it, borrow it, invest it, and make it grow for you.

Instead of sitting around watching TV, surfing the Internet, or wasting time with social media, try watching YouTube videos about money, investing, business, and building wealth.

Watch videos and read books by Dave Ramsey and Suze Orman. These two money gurus are two of the best in the world for learning about how to get out of debt and manage your money.

It amazes me how people will take golf or tennis lessons, but they don't even think of taking money lessons. How many of us have a money coach? We have a dentist, doctor, and an insurance agent, but most of us never sit down and talk to a financial services professional. We love to read books like *The Lord of the Rings* and *Fifty Shades of Gray*. How many books on wealth building and investing do you read each year? We enjoy going to ethnic festivals for their food, music, and culture. When was the last time you attended a seminar or conference on financial freedom, investing, or personal improvement? We love watching fictional people live their lives on TV shows. When was the last time you watched a show, movie, or YouTube video that will help you improve your own real life?

Below is a list of books to help with your education about how money works:

- *The Richest Man in Babylon,* by George S. Clason
- *The Complete Guide to Money,* by Dave Ramsey
- *Rich Dad, Poor Dad,* by Robert Kiyosaki
- *The Money Class,* by Suze Orman

Save 5-10% of everything you earn

If you are not saving any money, this is something you need to change immediately. I know you might be wondering how you can do this if you are living paycheck to paycheck. Look at it this way. If your paycheck was reduced by 5% tomorrow, you would have no choice but to live off 5% less money. This is the way you need to approach saving money.

If you read any book about personal finance and money management, they all contain the following statement: *Pay yourself first.*

Open a savings account immediately and pay yourself first, depositing 5% off the top of everything you earn. Use this account only for saving money and nothing else. This is a fund you never touch. As soon as you get paid, deposit 5% of your take-home pay in this account. Whatever you have left after you set aside your savings is what you live on. Pay all your mandatory bills next—these are the things you can't live without like rent money, car payment, groceries, healthcare, and heating and electric bills.

I am positive there is something you can do without to enable you to save that 5% from each paycheck.

I hope you get the real message I am trying to convey in this chapter. If you want to change your life and become rich, then you must change what you are doing with your money.

ASSET #6: HEALTH

PURSUE GOOD HEALTH

"It is health that is real wealth and not the pieces of gold and silver."
—Mahatma Gandhi

I saved the chapter on health for last because I felt if I discussed it first, most people might stop reading, thinking, "I thought this book would give me the secrets to fast and easy riches! What does health have to do with that?"

But, really, maintaining your health is foundational to getting rich and realizing your dream life. Health is the foundation of all the other Life Assets. Without good health you can't leverage your other superpowers. Every concept I discussed in this book is important when it comes to changing your life—it would be hard to choose one as more important than the next. It's important to be ready for change and to write down your goals and plans. You need to have a successful mindset, surround yourself with the right people, value your time, become a lifelong learner, and take control of your finances. However, without your physical and mental health, you might not have the energy to do any of the above.

It is almost impossible to change your life and become rich if you don't have good health. How you treat your body has as much to do with changing your life and becoming rich as all the other advice in this book.

Entire books have been written about diet, exercise, and emotional health. This one chapter alone cannot do justice to these important topics, but this book would be incomplete in helping you if I did not at least discuss my own lessons regarding good health. I can't express enough how important my health is in my own pursuit of financial freedom. Success and good health go together. I am fully convinced that you cannot meet your goals without first having good health.

When you look at the best professional athletes in the world, they treat their minds and bodies like temples. When they step on the playing field, they want to deliver peak performance. Your life is no different from theirs. You might think that trying to become rich has nothing to do with physical stamina, but it does. Your physical and mental stamina will be critical if you want to go from being poor to being rich. If you want to become rich you must have the physical and mental state of a great athlete. Changing your life and becoming rich will be challenging. At times it will be mentally and physically exhausting.

Becoming rich and pursuing change requires:

- Being motivated.
- Having energy throughout the day.
- Staying focused.
- Having a positive attitude.

- Working extra hours.
- Being creative.
- Avoiding illness.
- Committing to change and sacrifice.

If you are exhausted because you have poor diet and sleep habits, then you are not going to want to make the sacrifices and put in the time it takes to change. You will have a negative attitude and zero motivation. You won't get up early to read, study, exercise, or pursue goals. You will be tired, and you'll just keep putting off working on your goals until the next day.

What is good health?

Now that you understand how important a healthy lifestyle is, let's discuss what defines good health and what you can do to pursue and maintain it. I am not a nutritionist, physician, or personal trainer but I have played sports my entire life, worked out in gyms, and continue to play competitive tennis. Even though I've had many healthy periods in my life, I have also experienced what a poor diet, no exercise, and poison can do to my mind and body. I've lived both ways and I'm qualified to say that living healthy is better and more effective to living a successful life. Below is a list of the most important habits and traits that lead to good health:

- Good quality sleep.
- Proper diet.
- Regular hydration.
- Regular exercise.
- Avoiding stress and toxic people.

- Avoiding poisons.

If you can improve these areas in your life, you'll feel and look better. Every day your health will get better. This will only increase your chances of changing your life to become rich.

Good quality sleep

I believe sleep is the most important element in changing your life. Without healthy sleep, it will be hard to change your life and become rich. Sleep is the way your mind and body recharge and repair themselves. Your brain and body are like cell phone batteries. You recharge your entire being with a good night of sleep.

Lack of sleep or chronic insomnia can be debilitating. Insomnia causes employers billions of dollars in lost productivity every year and causes numerous health problems. About ten years ago I was exiting an eight-year relationship with a girlfriend, and my business partnership was starting down the road of what would become a three-year business divorce. The stress from these events was tremendous. I could not sleep more than a couple of hours a night. I had chronic insomnia. I was not able to do anything else with my life. I was barely able to keep my full-time job. I had hives all over my body, constant nosebleeds, terrible cramps in my feet and legs, and even dental problems. The stress was ruining my life. Eventually I moved on emotionally from these stressful events, but it was still another year before my sleep returned to normal levels. I know what a lack of sleep can do to a person. Without sleep, both your focus and your commitment to change your life go right out the window.

When I get eight hours of good quality sleep, my

productivity and creativity the next day is incredible. I spend more time writing books and creating seminars. I spend more time working on real estate deals. I am happy all day long. If someone told me that for a $10,000 annual fee, I could be guaranteed eight hours of uninterrupted sleep every night, I would gladly pay that fee. I know I would make the $10,000 back several times every year with my increased productivity and creativity.

For me, exceptional sleep means sleeping at least seven hours per night without tossing and turning or lying awake for hours at a time. I'm not a sleep therapist, but I have discovered some tips that might help you consistently have a good night's sleep.

First, make sure you are sleeping in a cool, dark, and quiet bedroom. Studies show that you will sleep better under these conditions. Also, go to bed and wake up at the same time as much as possible. Going to bed at the same time every night and waking the same time every morning will reset your sleep clock and you will start to fall asleep easier and stay asleep longer.

If you go to bed and you can't fall asleep, don't lie there tossing and turning. You will only make things worse and you will train your mind to lie awake in bed. If you can't fall asleep after 15 or 20 minutes, then get out of bed and do something else for an hour. When I can't sleep because something is bothering me, I get up and write down what I will do the next day to solve the problem. This helps me settle down and get back to sleep.

When you go to bed, try some controlled breathing exercises or meditation techniques. Inhale deeply and exhale deeply ten times. Then mediate for 5 to 10 minutes. This helps me settle down if I've had a busy or stressful day.

Don't eat or drink late at night before going to bed. I

don't eat after dinner anymore. I find that if I eat late at night, I have trouble falling and staying asleep. Eating a healthy diet will also help you sleep better. Foods that are high in fat, dairy, caffeine, and inflammatory ingredients are going to keep you up at night. You don't want to go to bed at night with a bloated stomach because you just ate a large pizza.

Make sure you invest in a first-rate mattress and a therapeutic pillow as they have an enormous impact on the quality of your sleep. With mattresses, you get what you pay for, so don't skimp on these items. Again, sleeping well has a huge impact on how well you're able to change your life. I've realized how quality sleep has helped me succeed and change my life in so many ways. That's why sleep has now become one of my biggest priorities—it has set me on the path to success.

If you truly aren't sleeping well, I recommend that you see your doctor to make sure you aren't suffering from a medical condition that is affecting your sleep. You could also try reading one or more of the many good books on the market that help you understand and plan for quality sleep. We will talk about diet, exercise, and stress later in this chapter. These are all factors in promoting good sleep.

Food

 I used to live my life eating junk food that was inflammatory to my body. Now I live it eating healthy food. The difference in the way I have felt during these two phases of my life is extraordinary. Eating quality food is like putting high-octane gasoline in a race car. Changing

your life and becoming rich is like running a competitive race. If you want your race car to excel and win the race, you'd better take care of it. You need to give it top quality fuel. Food is your fuel for success. Unhealthy food brings about an inferior performance while healthy food will allow you to give your peak performance. It is that simple. If you want to change your life and become rich, you need to eat healthy food.

I have played sports my entire life, and I still play competitive tennis. At one time a few years back, however, I almost stopped playing tennis. I'd found myself struggling every time I played, getting completely winded within 20 minutes with sweat pouring off my body. I had Plantar fasciitis in both feet, an inflamed rotator cuff, tennis elbow, and arthritis in my wrist.

Beyond the tennis court, I was completely exhausted by 5 p.m. every day. I had trouble putting in an eight-hour workday and would arrive home, exhausted, crashing on the couch.

I assumed it was just my age catching up with me and thought maybe it was time to give up competitive sports. In hindsight, that would have been a terrible decision.

One day I was playing tennis with my friend and, after ten minutes, I was on one knee trying to catch my breath. My friend told me I really needed to go see a doctor. I took his advice and went to see a cardiologist for a complete stress test. The verdict: there was nothing medically wrong with me.

A few days later, I heard about a book that had just come out. It detailed the types of food that cause inflammation in the body. I realized my entire diet was made of these inflammatory foods: dairy, gluten, processed sugar, sodium, processed meat, and other processed foods.

My diet consisted of a loaf of bread every two days, four daily pints of milk, and ice cream and cookies every evening. Most of my lunches and dinners were made up of pasta, gnocchi, and pierogis. I was still working as a real estate agent at the time, driving around in my car all day. During my driving for work, I'd stop by the convenience store or a coffee shop for flavored mochas and pastries. I also met clients and vendors for breakfast several times a week, where I would consume bacon, sausage, or ham. Almost everything I was consuming had some form of dairy, gluten, processed sugar, sodium, or processed meat in it. I was a walking body of inflammation.

I decided to try to avoid inflammatory foods and see if it helped me feel better. I switched from dairy milk to almond or coconut milk. I went from eating ice cream every night to only once a week. I gave up the stops at convenience stores for sugary coffees and snacks. I gave up cookies. I switched to rice-based pasta and gluten-free bread products. I limited my bacon consumption to once every two weeks. I tried not to give up everything I loved— I was just striving for more moderation. Let's be real here, I am not going to live without bacon and ice cream!

The new diet changed my health in an extreme way. Within four short weeks of changing my eating habits, all the conditions from which I'd suffered all disappeared. I couldn't believe it! The pain in my feet, elbow, wrist, and shoulder were completely gone. I was able to work 12-hour days without feeling tired. I could play five sets of tennis without getting winded or overheated. It has been four years since I made the changes to my diet and I have never felt better in all my life. I haven't had a single relapse in any of my past conditions or ailments. They seem to be permanently gone. I know this sounds hard to believe. When I tell people this story, they look at me with disbelief.

There are dozens of books on healthy eating and anti-inflammatory diets. Magazine and blog articles abound that cover healthy eating. Start to make healthy eating a regular part of your life. You will feel better, have a positive attitude, sleep better, and increase your motivation to succeed. If you want to change your life and become rich, you must improve your diet. You need both your mind and body to support your success and goals.

Water

Another subject that most people think has nothing to do with becoming rich is staying hydrated by drinking plenty of water throughout the day. How much water you drink also can affect how you look and feel. Staying properly hydrated is an essential part of maintaining a healthy body and keeping your brain at optimum performance. Your brain is like the engine in a race car. If the engine is rusty or overheating, then the car breaks down and the driver can't finish the race. Water to your brain is like oil to a car. Our brains are 83% water. Brains that aren't hydrated won't operate at peak performance. Our brains drive our motivation, happiness level, and focus.

Speaking of your brain, did you know that avocados, purple grapes, fish oil, and blueberries can reduce plaque in the brain that can contribute to Alzheimer's and early onset memory loss? Many case studies prove how diets rich in fish oils can reverse brain damage. So, in addition to keeping your brain hydrated, consider also how to nourish your brain with healthy foods.

When I started to focus on drinking water in the morning and throughout the day, my remaining ulcerative colitis symptoms disappeared. Also, my tennis game improved. Back when I adopted an anti-inflammatory diet to improve my physical stamina on the tennis court, I also started to focus on my level of hydration. Much of my lack of stamina was due to a poor diet, but it was also due to being dehydrated. These days, I always make sure I show up to the tennis court with plenty of water in my system and extra water to drink while I am playing. My on-court stamina improved dramatically when I began to drink plenty of water during the hours leading up to a tennis match.

Numerous professional athletes start their day by consuming water on an empty stomach before they do

anything else. I can honestly say I feel more awake and vibrant when I start my day with a pint of filtered water.

If you drink at least eight to ten glasses

of water every day, it flushes all the toxins and helps your body to function properly. A well-known health regimen involving water is Japanese water therapy, which helps to clean your stomach and boost your digestive system. Japanese traditional medicine recommends drinking water right after waking up in the morning. It is believed that drinking water on an empty stomach when you first wake up not only promotes weight loss by smoothing out your digestive system but also helps in treating various health problems.

Japanese water therapy helps relieve stress, promotes weight loss, and ensures a strong digestive system. Most of all, it keeps you energetic throughout the day. Drinking enough water during the day also revs up your metabolism.

If you want to try Japanese water therapy, drink about 20 ounces of water when you first wake up, even before you brush your teeth. The water should be at room temperature—not chilled. Try to abstain from eating or drinking anything else for 45 minutes after the water, then have your breakfast. Also, a part of this practice is to avoid eating or drinking anything for about two hours after every meal of the day. Of course, if you have an issue that prevents you from drinking that much water at one time, you can drink what you can and try to gradually increase to 20 ounces eventually.

Research has shown that drinking water upon waking has many health benefits, such as improved digestion, better complexion, and reduced wrinkles. People have also found that they have better energy throughout the day, reduced symptoms from diseases, and an easier time at weight loss. Japanese water therapy not only flushes the toxins from your body but also promotes your immune system and just generally makes you happier.

Exercise

If I had a dime for every article, study, or news show talking about how exercise promotes longevity and reduces disease and stress, I would be rich from that alone. As I mentioned earlier, I have played sports and worked out most of my life, except for a couple of time periods when I was less active. I spent the first ten years after I graduated from college without a habit of exercise and then again when I was going through the bad breakup and business divorce I mentioned earlier. During these periods, I also experienced the worst health of my life. I looked unhealthy, felt terrible, and had numerous health problems. My friends and family often told me I looked sick. My stomach problems were so bad that I was hospitalized for five days. I had joint problems and was tired all the time.

During the more active periods of my life, my near perfect health has enabled me to accomplish my educational, business, and financial goals. Right now, I'm playing tennis three times a week. I have no health problems and people tell me I look great.

I am positive that, if you include regular exercise in your life, you will greatly improve your chances of changing your life and becoming rich. Studies show that the human body is made for movement. Exercise and movement promote good health. I know from my own experience that exercise improves every area of life that you will need to become successful.

Some of the many benefits of exercise include:

- Healthy digestive system.
- Healthy weight.
- An increase in bone density.
- An increase in muscle mass.
- Good sleep.
- Lack of stress.
- A better appearance.
- Improved sex drive.
- Better looking skin.
- Help with conditions like heart disease and diabetes.
- A healthy brain.
- Boost in confidence and self-esteem.
- Healthier joints and reduced back problems.
- Improved circulation.

Avoid stress and toxic people

Stress can derail you from accomplishing your goals, cause major health problems, and even kill you. I have had a couple of very stressful time periods in my life, so I know what it can do to a person if it goes unchecked. If you want to change your life and become rich, then you must be able to identify stress, eliminate it or counteract its effects on you.

Below is a list of just a few sources of stress:

- Aggravating boss or coworkers.
- Bad finances.
- Toxic people in your life.

- Watching and listening to negative media.
- Health problems experienced by you or your loved ones.
- Abusive life partners, siblings, or parents.
- Bad diet.
- Lack of exercise.
- Putting poisons into your body.

Handling stress is like all the other subjects in this book. The solution is not one thing alone but rather meshes with all aspects of your lifestyle. If you read and implement the knowledge in the chapters on surrounding yourself with the right people, guarding your time, or becoming financially responsible, then you are essentially reading about how to remove stress from your life.

This is a list of the most important ways to reduce stress from your life:

1. Find role models and positive people to be around.
2. Get abusive people out of your life.
3. Change jobs if you aren't happy.
4. Eat a healthy diet.
5. Stop watching violent or negative TV.
6. Get off social media if just used for entertainment.
7. Get regular exercise.
8. Get out of debt and start saving money.
9. Stay hydrated.
10. Get eight hours of sleep.

The way you take care of your body will ultimately help you better achieve your goals of becoming successful. If you think of your body as a tool that needs quality sleep, a proper diet, daily hydration, and regular exercise, you'll feel good, look good, and be able to rise to any height you desire. However, if you don't take care of yourself, you'll drop into an abyss of defeat.

I want you to have a great life full of opportunity and growth. The bottom line is this: if you want to accomplish your goals, your mind and body must be in peak condition. It doesn't matter if you are an athlete, student, or entrepreneur, you must have good health to succeed in any area of life.

FINAL THOUGHTS

This book is called *How to Get Rich in 5 Hours*. How is it possible my parents worked for a combined 80 years yet they were poor? I spent 20 years in the corporate world as an engineer and software developer, owned a bar, a nightclub, and profitable real estate investments and I wound up poor and sick. How can someone get rich in five hours when my parents and I could not do it for a combined effort of 100 years? This can't be possible!

If I called this book The Belief Systems, Knowledge, and Concepts Used by the World's Wealthiest People to Build and Protect Wealth, you probably wouldn't buy it. *How to get Rich in 5 Hours* is a much sexier and more interesting title. Is it accurate and true?

Think and Grow Rich by Napoleon Hill should really have the title Think, Plan, and Accomplish Anything You Want. Again, that title probably would not be one of the world's best-selling nonfiction books of all time. I once read a book entitled, *How to Be a Millionaire*. I purchased the book because the title was just what I wanted to hear at the time. Let's face it, who doesn't want to be a millionaire? I was totally jazzed by the title. What followed was a methodical, very structured system on how to live beneath your means, pay yourself first, save and invest your money in mutual funds for the long haul, and retire with a million dollars. I learned a lot from that book, and I was glad I read it. The title was true, just not what I was looking for. I wanted a million dollars now. I believe these books have accurate titles and have lived up to their billing.

The question you might be asking yourself right now is: will I be rich when I finish reading this book? As far as the five-hour time period is concerned, if you have the reading speed of the average adult, five hours is the amount of time it will take to read this book. A typical nonfiction book has around 50-60,000 words or around 175-225 pages. The average adult reads anywhere from 200-300 words per minute. Let us be conservative and say the average adult reads 225 words per minute. If you read a 60,000-word book at a rate of 225 words per minute, it would take the average adult approximately 266 minutes or 4.44 hours to read the book. Again, let's be conservative and round that number up to five hours to read this book.

If you read this book in approximately five hours and you truly embrace the belief systems and implement the knowledge, habits, and concepts, I believe you will be just as rich as any wealthy person living today. As far as I am concerned, you will be rich. The numbers in your bank account are not important. Money, assets, and toys are results of leveraging your six Life Assets correctly. The income and net worth will follow as you go forward and think and act like the rich person you want to be. It is that simple. Since I have embraced the mindset and lifestyle of a rich person, my annual income, net worth, and the number of cash flow producing assets I own have grown every year.

Remember, whatever you spend a lot of time doing, that is what you will be good at. I spend all my time thinking and acting like a rich person and leveraging my six Life Assets. The result is every day my net worth and income keep growing.

After I graduated from college with my degree in electrical engineering, I worked as an engineer outside of Boston at a semiconductor company. One of our tactics for competing with other semiconductor companies was to purchase their products, take the product apart, see how it worked, and then try to design a better version. This is a common practice today amongst competitors in all types of industries. Taking apart the competitor's product is known as reverse engineering. Redesigning a better version of the product is known as reengineering the product.

This book is about reverse engineering your life and reengineering a version that will empower you to obtain everything you desire. If you want to change and become rich, then you must deconstruct your life and reconstruct the life of a person who thinks and acts like a rich person. If you do this, you will become rich.

You must change what you do with your six Life Assets. These truly are superpowers if you use them wisely. You must change what you eat, drink, watch, and listen to. You might have to change jobs or careers along the way. You will almost certainly have to change who you trust and spend time with. Changing what you do with your time and money will be necessary on your new journey.

I promise you if you take this journey, every aspect of your life will improve. Being in control of your emotions, health, happiness, and financial situation is an incredible feeling. I love getting out of bed every day and spending my day creating abundance, prosperity, and wealth and sharing it with people like you. It is a great feeling to realize that nothing in life is about fate or luck. We are in complete control of how we live our lives and what life brings to us. Go forward working smart and hard to bring value to other people and you will be rewarded for the rest of your life.

You have the same God-given talent and potential as everyone else. You can become or do anything you want. You can obtain everything life has to offer. Today in the world there is more abundance, opportunity, and wealth than ever before and there is no reason or excuse for you not to acquire your share of it. I wish you massive change, success, and happiness.

"What we are is God's gift to us, what we become is our gift to God."

Made in the USA
Monee, IL
10 June 2020